THE WEALTH YOU BUILD

A Lifetime of Financial Wisdom

Jimmy T. Singh, CPA

This book is intended to provide general information on the subjects it covers. It is not intended as, and should not be relied upon for, individualized financial, legal, tax, or investment advice. The author is a CPA and independent financial consultant, but this book is not a substitute for personalized advice from a qualified professional familiar with your specific circumstances. Laws, tax rules, contribution limits, and other figures referenced in this book change over time; readers should verify current rules before acting on any information contained here. Personal examples, decisions, and results described throughout this book reflect the author's own experience and are shared for illustration only; they are not a guarantee or prediction of similar results for any reader.

First Edition

ISBN: 979-8-9971830-1-1

Published by Jimmy T. Singh

Long Island, New York

Printed in the United States of America.

To my grandson —

May you ask not only how much you have, but what it is for. May this book be a compass as you build the life that is yours to build.

To my wife —

Whose quiet partnership made every word of this book, and every year that came before it, possible.

Table of Contents

Introduction i

Part One — Your Relationship with Money

Chapter 1 — Money Is a Tool, Not the Destination 1
Chapter 2 — What Financial Independence Really Buys You 7
Chapter 3 — Living Below Your Means 13
Chapter 4 — Building Wealth Quietly 19

Part Two — The Habits That Build Wealth

Chapter 5 — The Habits That Build Financial Security 27
Chapter 6 — The Cost of Debt 37
Chapter 7 — The Power of Consistent Investing 43
Chapter 8 — Time, Your Greatest Financial Asset 51

Part Three — Protecting Your Financial Future

Chapter 9 — Health Is Part of Wealth 59
Chapter 10 — Building an Emergency Fund 67
Chapter 11 — Insurance, Protecting What You've Built 75
Chapter 12 — Why Smart People Still Get Money Wrong 83

Part Four — Making Retirement Work

Chapter 13 — Understanding Social Security Before You Claim 95
Chapter 14 — Retirement Is Freedom, Not the End of Purpose 101
Chapter 15 — Turning a Lifetime of Savings into a Lifetime of Income 109
Chapter 16 — Keeping More of What You Earn 119

Part Five — Beyond Wealth

Chapter 17 — Teaching the Next Generation About Money 129
Chapter 18 — The Legacy You Leave 137
Chapter 19 — Wealth in Service of a Life Well Lived 143

Appendix — Retirement Planning Worksheets 149
Notes on Sources 151
About the Author 159

Introduction

I did not set out to write a book about money.

I spent nearly forty years in public accounting and corporate finance, including more than a decade as a Corporate Controller. I left corporate life at sixty-one, not because I was finished working, but because the financial foundation I had built gave me the freedom to choose what came next.

What came next, among other things, was writing. This is the second book to emerge from that second act and, in many ways, the one I most wanted to write from the beginning because it is the most practical. It is not a memoir. It is a roadmap built from the habits, mistakes, and decisions of an actual financial life rather than a theoretical one.

This book is organized around a simple idea, stated in the first chapter and returned to in the last: money is a tool, not the destination. Everything in between, including the habits that build wealth, the protections that guard it, the decisions that carry you through retirement, and the legacy that outlasts it, grows from that one idea, examined from five different angles. Money matters because of the security, freedom, and choices it can make possible, not because of the number itself.

Throughout this book, I distinguish between what I actually did and what I would recommend more broadly. Where the two differ, I say so. I have largely avoided pinning the book to a particular year's contribution limits, tax thresholds, or other figures.

Those numbers change, sometimes significantly, and what is accurate today may not remain accurate for long. Instead, I have focused on the reasoning behind the decisions, the why underneath the what, because sound reasoning remains useful long after a particular rule has changed.

I am a CPA and an independent financial consultant, but this book is not a substitute for professional advice tailored to your own circumstances. It is an account of the principles that guided my financial life, offered in the hope that some of them will prove useful in yours.

What I have learned is that managing money well has very little to do with being clever. It comes from seeing your position clearly, choosing a sound plan, and following it consistently long enough for the results to appear. I hope this book helps you do exactly that.

PART ONE

YOUR RELATIONSHIP WITH MONEY

CHAPTER ONE

Money Is a Tool, Not the Destination

Most people spend their lives believing that money is the goal. It is not. Money is one of the most useful tools we possess, but it is a poor destination. A tool exists to help us build something. It has no meaning on its own. A hammer left in a drawer builds nothing. A dollar left unspent, unused, and unconsidered does the same. The real question is not how much money you have. It is what that money allows you to build, and for whom.

After nearly forty years in finance, I walked away from a successful career before I had to. Friends assumed the decision was about retirement. It was not. It was about freedom.

The moment itself was quieter than people might expect. We had been working from home since 2020, and toward the end of the pandemic, I realized I was not going back into the office. I sat down with my wife and walked her through the plan I had already been carrying in my head for a long time. She listened, and asked me to sit with the decision a little longer before making it final. I had already thought it through. I was ready. I did not mention any of it to my colleagues until after the decision was made. Once it was, I informed them that I would be leaving corporate life.

Years of disciplined saving had finally given me something far more valuable than a paycheck: the ability to choose. Choose what I wanted to do, and how, and when, for the remainder of the years I still have while I still have them. I did not always think this way. Like many young professionals, I once believed that earning more would eventually eliminate financial worry. Experience taught me otherwise.

Over those years, I learned that numbers tell only part of the story. Behind every balance sheet, budget, and financial statement were people making decisions shaped as much by their beliefs about money as by the money itself. I remember presenting financial statements after another successful year. The numbers were excellent. Revenue had grown, expenses were under control, and cash reserves were healthy. Yet the discussion around the table was dominated by fear, as though no amount of profit would ever feel secure enough. Walking out of that meeting, I realized something I never forgot. Financial success does not automatically create financial peace. Those are two very different things, and I have watched people confuse them ever since.

Ask someone why they want more money, and listen closely to the answer. Rarely does anyone say that they want the money itself. They want security. They want freedom. They want the opportunity to try something new without fear of losing everything. They want peace of mind when they lie awake at night. They want the ability to care for their children, their parents, or a cause that matters to them. Notice that not one of those things is money. Every one of them is something money can help provide, if it is managed with intention. Money is the means. It was never meant to be the end.

This distinction sounds simple, almost obvious, when stated plainly. Yet very few people live as though they believe it. I have talked with many people over the years who worried constantly about things that, set against the whole of a life, were minor drops in a much larger bucket. That kind of persistent, small-scale worry has a way of preventing people from stepping back, seeing the larger picture, and considering how to live well. I believe that failure to see it, more than any lack of money itself, is one of the real reasons people fail to live a good life.

A carpenter never mistakes his hammer for the home he is trying to build. Money deserves the same perspective. It is powerful, but its power has limits. It cannot buy wisdom. It cannot purchase integrity. It cannot create love, trust, gratitude, or inner peace. No amount of savings can substitute for a marriage built on trust, and no investment return can replace the quiet satisfaction of raising a child who becomes a person of integrity. These things come from somewhere else entirely, from choices made over years, from patience, from love, from faith, and from character.

What money can do, when it is managed wisely, is protect those things. It can protect your health by allowing you access to care when you need it, without the added burden of financial fear layered on top of a medical one. It can protect your relationships by removing the corrosive stress that so often accompanies debt and scarcity. It can protect your sleep by giving you room to walk away from a job, a deal, or a demand that conflicts with your values because you are not trapped by financial necessity. Money, handled with intention, does not create the good things in life. It creates the space in which those good things are free to grow.

I think of money the way I think of a well-built foundation. No one builds a home because they admire the foundation. They build it because of the life that will be lived above it. A strong foundation goes largely unnoticed when it is doing its job well. It is only when it is neglected, when it cracks or shifts beneath the weight of the home, that everyone suddenly understands how much it mattered all along. Money works the same way. When it is managed with discipline, it quietly supports the life being built above it. When it is neglected or mistaken for the point of the whole exercise, the entire structure becomes unstable.

Money is a wonderful servant but a terrible master. This reframing matters because it changes the questions you ask yourself. Instead of asking, “How do I get more money?” the more useful question becomes, “What am I trying to build, and what role should money play in building it?” Instead of measuring your progress by a number in an account, you begin measuring it by the life that number is making possible. That shift, small as it sounds, changes decisions in ways that compound over decades. It changes how you spend, how you save, how you invest, and eventually how you think about work itself, about retirement, and about what you hope to leave behind.

None of this is meant to diminish the discipline required to build financial security. Living below your means, avoiding unnecessary debt, and investing consistently over time are not easy habits, and the chapters that follow will address each of them directly. But none of those habits will hold much meaning if you have not first settled the question this chapter asks. Before you can build wealth with purpose, you have to understand what wealth is for.

When I look back over my own life, I do not remember my bank balances from thirty years ago. I remember raising our children, the opportunities my wife and I were able to give our family, the people who influenced me, and the freedom to make decisions that aligned with my values. Money made some of those things possible, but it was never the reason they mattered.

Money is not the destination. It never was. The moment we mistake money for the destination, we begin asking it to provide things it was never meant to provide. It cannot satisfy a longing for purpose or replace the relationships that give life meaning. It can support those things, but it cannot become them. When money becomes a tool instead of the destination, something remarkable happens. It begins to buy not possessions, but choices. And choices are the beginning of financial independence, which is exactly where we turn next.

CHAPTER TWO

What Financial Independence Really Buys You

Financial independence is often measured in dollars. It is better measured in choices.

Most people think of financial independence as a number. Reach it, and you are free. Fall short, and you are not. I understand the appeal of that thinking. Numbers are concrete. They can be calculated, tracked, and celebrated when they are finally reached. But after nearly four decades of seeing that pursuit play out in my own life and in the lives of colleagues and clients, I have come to believe that the number itself was never the point. Financial independence is not about reaching a figure on a statement. It is about gaining the freedom to make choices based on your values rather than your obligations.

That distinction matters more than it sounds. A person can reach an impressive number and still feel trapped, because the habits and fears that built the number never loosened their grip. Another person can be years from any conventional definition of "enough" and still feel free, because they have already begun making decisions from a place of security rather than scarcity. Financial independence, properly understood, is less a finish line than a widening of what is possible.

For one person, financial independence may mean leaving a job they no longer enjoy. For another, it may mean caring for an aging parent, starting a business, volunteering, or simply sleeping better at night. The amount differs from person to person. The freedom underneath it is the same.

What does that shift actually buy you? In my experience, it comes down to a handful of things, and none of them are the money itself.

The first is peace of mind. When you have built a financial cushion, an unexpected expense stops being a crisis and becomes an inconvenience. A car repair, a medical bill, a period of reduced income: these things still happen, but they no longer threaten to unravel everything you have built. That peace is difficult to put a number on, but anyone who has lived without it, and later lived with it, knows exactly what it is worth.

The second is freedom of choice, particularly around work. Financial independence does not necessarily mean you stop working. For most people, it means something more specific. It means you can choose work because it is meaningful, challenging, or aligned with your values, rather than choosing it because you have no other option. The difference is profound, even for someone who continues working every day of their life.

The third is time. Time to spend with family. Time to invest in your own health. Time to learn something new, to serve a cause you believe in, or simply to slow down. Money cannot manufacture more hours in a day, but the freedom that comes from financial independence changes how those hours can be spent. Fewer of them are consumed by financial anxiety or by work taken solely out of necessity.

The fourth is purpose. Without the constant pressure of financial survival, you are free to pursue what actually matters to you, rather than what simply pays the bills. Money still matters. It simply stops being the only voice in the room when you are deciding what to do with your life.

The fifth is dignity. There is a real difference between being financially prepared and being financially dependent, whether that dependence is on an employer, on debt, or on circumstances beyond your control. Financial independence restores a kind of quiet confidence, the sense that you are standing on your own foundation rather than someone else's.

Taken together, these are what financial independence really buys. The money simply makes them possible.

I did not fully understand these five things as separate ideas when I lived through the decision I am about to describe. I understood them only afterward, looking back. At the time, it was simply the decision that felt right.

I want to tell you about a decision I made that illustrates this better than any list of principles could. At one point in my career, I left a higher-paying position to accept one that paid less. On paper, it looked like the wrong move. Fewer dollars, less prestige attached to the title, and colleagues who quietly questioned why anyone would walk away from a role most people were working toward. But I was not looking at the paper. Colleagues never said it directly, but the implication was clear enough: stepping down to an entry-level senior accountant role, after where I had been, looked like moving backward. What they could not see was what I saw. The organization was in healthcare, a field I already knew well from my years auditing health and hospital agencies. It was a natural fit, and my own research told me it was a strong long-term opportunity. I was not settling for less. I was choosing a better future over a bigger paycheck. That one decision eventually led to opportunities I could never have predicted, including leadership roles, financial security, and ultimately the freedom to write, consult, spend more time with my family, and choose how I wanted to live the next chapter of my life.

I want to be careful here, because I am not telling you this story to suggest that everyone should take a pay cut, or that income does not matter. It does. I did not have a large cushion of savings set aside that made this decision easy or risk-free. Most of what we had saved by that point had already gone into buying our first home, and our retirement savings, while consistent from the very start of my career, were still modest. What made the decision possible was not a stockpile of cash. It was clarity. I could see, with real conviction, that this offered better long-term prospects than staying where I was. There was nothing reckless about it. I was making a judgment call about the years ahead, backed by conviction rather than cash. That decision changed the course of my career.

That is the heart of what financial independence really provides. Hard decisions do not disappear. What changes is that you get to make them on your own terms.

Many people misunderstand financial independence because they define it too narrowly. For many, it means simply, "I never have to work again." I would gently challenge that definition. For me, financial independence has meant something closer to this: I can choose the work I do because I want to do it, not because I have no other choice. That is a very different kind of freedom than simply not working. It is the freedom to keep contributing, keep building, and keep engaging with meaningful work, without that work being dictated by fear of what happens if the paycheck stops.

I have seen the same thing from the other direction as well. Over the years, I met people who had accumulated significant wealth and still could not walk away from a job, a role, or a decision they knew was wrong for them, because some part of their identity, or their fear, kept them tethered to income they did not actually need. Financial independence, in the truest sense, never arrived for them, no matter what the balance in their accounts said. The number was there. The freedom was not.

This is why I encourage you to think of financial independence less as a destination and more as a widening set of options. Every dollar you save, every debt you avoid, every dollar you invest consistently over time does not just add to a balance. It adds to your options. It gives you a little more room to say no to something that does not serve you, and a little more room to say yes to something that does. Some people reach a point where those options are so wide that continuing to work becomes entirely optional. Others, like myself, reach a point where the options are wide enough to choose a different kind of work, a different pace, or a different purpose, without the choice being driven by financial desperation.

None of this happens overnight. It is worth saying plainly that the freedom I have described was not the product of a single decision or a single fortunate year. Even the earliest of these decisions, choosing a lower-paying role because it mattered more, was made possible by habits I had only been practicing for barely two years at that point, not decades. The decades came later, as those same habits were sustained and compounded across the rest of my career. Each one, taken individually, may not feel significant.

Together, sustained over years, they are what built the foundation beneath every meaningful choice I have since been able to make.

Financial independence is not the absence of work. It is the absence of financial fear. It lets you answer to your own judgment instead of to whatever your circumstances happen to require. No one purchases that freedom overnight. It accumulates through thousands of ordinary financial decisions, each one bringing you a little closer to a life where money serves you rather than controls you. Financial independence does not free you from work. It frees you from compromising who you are.

The question, then, is how that kind of freedom is actually built. Like almost everything worthwhile in finance, it begins with small, consistent habits, repeated over many years, starting with the way you choose to live below what you earn.

CHAPTER THREE

Living Below Your Means

As the previous chapter made clear, financial independence is built through small, consistent habits rather than in a single moment, and the first of them is the simplest to state and the hardest to sustain: spend less than you earn. Most people believe financial success begins with earning more. In my experience, it begins much earlier, with learning to live on less than you make. That simple gap between income and spending becomes one of the most powerful forces in building financial security. When spending exceeds income instead, the difference does not disappear. It either depletes savings or becomes debt. And debt rarely stays where it started. The more debt a person carries, the greater the risk a lender sees in lending to them, and the higher the interest rate that lender is likely to charge. What begins as a small gap between income and spending can compound into a much larger burden, not because of one bad decision, but because of the interest that keeps accumulating on top of it. Living below your means goes well beyond budgeting technique. It is the discipline that keeps that cycle from ever starting.

I have watched this go both ways over the course of my career, and the pattern is remarkably consistent. It rarely begins with a single reckless purchase. It begins gradually, one expense at a time, often driven by something entirely outside a person's own life.

We live in an environment saturated with marketing. Turn on the television, pick up your phone, and something is telling you that you need to stay at this hotel, drive this car, or live a certain kind of lifestyle, because that is apparently how everyone else is living. A neighbor buys a new car every three years, even though they barely drive it, and suddenly there is a quiet pressure to do the same. A colleague posts photographs from a resort, and within days a dozen other people are pricing the same trip, not because they had planned it, but because the images made the absence of it feel like a lack. I have seen this pull people into spending far beyond what they earn, chasing a lifestyle that looks successful from the outside.

This is worth sitting with for a moment, because the pressure rarely feels like pressure while it is happening. It feels like simply keeping up, or treating yourself, or not wanting to fall behind. Very few people wake up and decide to go into debt. They make a series of individually reasonable-sounding purchases, each one justified in the moment, until the accumulation of those purchases becomes a monthly obligation they did not intend to create. The marketing around us is effective precisely because it rarely asks for a large decision all at once. It asks for a small one, repeatedly, until the small ones add up to something much larger.

Here is what most people do not realize. The people who appear to be living that lifestyle very often are not the people you should be comparing yourself to. Many of them are financing it. They have little in savings, they are carrying significant debt, and the appearance of success is often the most expensive thing they own. I have reviewed enough personal financial pictures over the years, directly and indirectly, to say with confidence that outward appearance and financial reality are frequently two very different things. Never compare your financial reality to someone else's public image. Living below your means starts with understanding that you do not have to live the way others appear to be living, especially when you have no real knowledge of what is happening behind their finances. What that appearance costs them, and how quickly it can unravel, is something we will return to later in this book.

I try to bring the decision back to two simple questions: can I afford this, and can I afford this without sacrificing my future goals? The first question is about today. The second is about tomorrow, and it is the one people skip most often. Many people can technically afford something today, but only by reducing the freedom they will have later. Not, did someone else just post about a trip. Not, does my neighbor have a newer car. Simply, can I afford this, and does affording it come at the cost of something I actually want more. If the answer to both is yes, that is one conversation. If either answer is no, the conversation is already over, regardless of what anyone else is doing.

My wife and I lived this out directly in our early years. We chose not to fly business class. A regular economy seat was perfectly comfortable, and it fit our budget. On cruises, in our early days, we booked a regular ocean view cabin, a little more than an interior room but nowhere near a suite, rather than anything more elaborate. It was not deprivation. I understood, watching our budget and our net worth grow year over year, that our income was staying ahead of our spending, and that gave me the confidence to know we were heading in the right direction. It was a decision, made deliberately, to spend within what we had rather than reach for what we had not yet earned. Looking back, I do not remember feeling deprived. I remember feeling confident that we were building something that would give us greater freedom later. Years later, once our finances allowed for it, we chose a suite. The difference was not that our values changed. The difference was that our means had grown to match the choice, and we no longer had to stretch to make it.

That progression matters more than the specific choice of cabin or seat. The lesson was never that a suite or a business class seat is wrong. The lesson is that the timing of the choice should follow your finances, not the other way around. Spending ahead of what you have earned, in an attempt to look like you have already arrived, is what quietly turns lifestyle into debt.

The opposite extreme deserves equal honesty, because I have seen it cause real harm as well. We had a neighbor who, at some point earlier in life, went through significant financial hardship. The experience left a lasting mark, and understandably so. It changed the way they thought about money going forward, even though by then they could genuinely afford far more than they allowed themselves. The response, years later, was to hoard almost everything. Money was saved and saved again, rarely spent, even on things that would have brought real joy or real comfort. Holding onto that cash so tightly kept them from doing things they had worked hard for and wanted to do, and that opportunity was lost. I understood where that instinct came from, but I never believed it was the healthier path either. We are given one life to live, and living in constant fear of spending, even when the means are genuinely there, is its own kind of imbalance. Financial wisdom lies in spending intentionally, not in spending nothing at all.

Both extremes, I have noticed, tend to come from the same place: letting something outside your own values dictate your financial decisions. For the person chasing a lifestyle, it is the fear of appearing to fall behind. For the person hoarding everything, it is the fear of a past struggle repeating itself. Living below your means, done well, is not driven by fear in either direction. It is driven by clarity about what you actually earn, what you actually value, and what you can afford, free of both the comparison and the anxiety.

Living below your means was never meant to mean living a joyless life. It means living intentionally. It means choosing to spend on the things that matter to you, the experiences and relationships and moments that bring real meaning, while declining to spend on things simply because someone else has them, or because you feel you need to impress someone who, frankly, is not thinking about you nearly as much as you imagine.

I think of it this way. Living below your means is not about restriction for its own sake. It is about creating a gap between what you earn and what you spend, deliberately and consistently, so that gap can become savings, and those savings can eventually become the freedom described in the previous chapter. Every dollar not spent chasing someone else's lifestyle is a dollar that remains available to build your own. Spend on what brings you real joy. Spend without regret when the means are there to support it. But let the decision be yours, built on your own finances and your own values, rather than a reaction to what everyone else appears to be doing.

That is the quiet discipline behind nearly every lasting fortune I have observed over the decades. Not extreme deprivation, and not extreme hoarding, but a steady, honest gap between income and spending, held consistently over time, and directed toward the life you actually want to build. The freedom to make meaningful choices tomorrow is built by the spending decisions you make today.

CHAPTER FOUR

Building Wealth Quietly

There is a difference between looking wealthy and being financially secure, and it is one of the most important distinctions in this entire book. Visible wealth is easy to display. A house, a car, a wardrobe, a vacation photograph: all of these can be arranged to suggest success, regardless of what actually stands behind them. Actual wealth is quieter. It does not need to be arranged, because it is not performing for anyone. The two sometimes coexist. More often than people realize, they do not.

I knew a family, years ago, that seemed to be building something unstoppable. They moved to a better neighborhood, into a more expensive home, chasing a better school system for their children. They renovated. They added a pool. They kept spending, year after year, on improvements that, I later realized, far exceeded what they actually earned. From the outside, everything about their life suggested a kind of quiet empire taking shape. We went to parties at their house that were genuinely lavish. What I did not see, and what almost no one around them saw, was that very little of it stood on anything solid. It was built on borrowed money, the kind of foundation that can take years to crack and then collapse far faster than anyone expects.

What had taken them a decade or more to build came apart in less than five years. The signs began to show. The home was sold, and the outward lifestyle contracted sharply. Retirement, which had once looked close, moved further away than it had ever been. What I had assumed was solidly built turned out to have no real financial foundation underneath it at all.

I do not share that story to judge anyone. Financial struggles are common, and they rarely announce themselves. I share it because it illustrates something I have seen play out in different forms throughout my career. One lost job, one illness, one business setback, or one unexpected expense is often all it takes to expose how little security actually existed beneath an appearance that looked, from the outside, entirely secure. The house is there until it is not. The pool is there until it has to be sold along with everything around it. Nothing about the appearance changes in the years leading up to that moment. What changes, when the moment finally arrives, is whether the people underneath it can absorb the shock, financially and otherwise.

Quiet wealth looks different, precisely because it is not built to be looked at. It may not attract attention. It may not photograph well. But it provides something visible wealth cannot: resilience. It gives a person savings, investments, manageable obligations, and the ability to absorb a setback without everything else falling apart. The value of that wealth is not that others can see it. The value is that it remains available when life becomes uncertain, which, sooner or later, it does for everyone.

I have often thought about what actually produces this kind of wealth, beyond the habits themselves. Saving and investing matter enormously, but the answer goes further than that. It comes from a particular set of qualities, developed over time, that shape how a person relates to money in the first place.

Patience comes first, because real wealth is almost always built over years, with very little to show for it in the early stages. A person without patience is easily pulled toward shortcuts, or toward spending that produces an immediate feeling of arrival, because waiting for the slower, real version feels unbearable by comparison. Discipline is what sustains that patience. Money has to be retained and invested rather than continually converted into lifestyle, which is simple to say and genuinely difficult to sustain once income begins to rise.

Then there is confidence, which is quieter than it sounds. A person who is secure does not need possessions to prove it, to themselves or to anyone else. Much of what passes for extravagant living has very little to do with the item being purchased and a great deal to do with the reassurance it is meant to provide. Closely related is a genuine independence from the opinions of others. Comparison is one of the greatest threats to long-term financial progress, as we discussed in the previous chapter, and it does not disappear once a person has built some wealth. If anything, it grows louder, because now there is more to compare and more people watching.

Last is clarity. A person building wealth quietly usually understands, with some specificity, what they are building toward and why it matters to them. That clarity makes it far easier to decline a purchase or a lifestyle upgrade that does not serve the actual goal, because the goal itself is clearly in view.

Building wealth quietly does not mean hiding success, refusing to enjoy life, or feeling guilty about spending. None of that is the point, and it would be its own kind of imbalance, the same one we discussed at the end of the last chapter. The point is simply that the financial decisions are not being made primarily for applause, approval, or appearance. A person building wealth quietly can still take the trip, still enjoy the nicer meal, still upgrade the home when the means genuinely support it. The difference is the reason behind the decision. Loud wealth is often designed to be seen. Quiet wealth is designed to endure.

Our own path looked very different, and it is worth telling here as a direct contrast. Early on, my wife and I bought a home that was comfortable, but modest by the standard of what we could technically have stretched for. That was a deliberate choice, not a limitation. We wanted a home we could afford while raising our two sons, keeping up with the mortgage, covering the ordinary costs of a family, and still setting money aside for the future. We were careful not to overextend ourselves, not because we expected anything to go wrong, but because we understood that a small setback, an unexpected expense, or a slower year should never turn into a scramble. No one can predict or fully protect against a genuine catastrophe. But the ordinary bumps of life, the ones every family eventually faces, we wanted to be able to absorb without disruption.

As my career progressed and our means grew, we did eventually upgrade, moving into a better neighborhood, in part because it offered better schools and better opportunities for our sons. But before we signed anything, I ran the numbers to make sure we could comfortably make the mortgage payments. My wife was working part time at that point, so I made sure we could live on my salary alone if we ever needed to, with our savings there to weather any short-term issue. Even that upgrade was made the same way the first home had been chosen: within what we could comfortably afford, without stretching, and without letting it become the first step toward a pattern of continually buying bigger. We have lived in that home for almost three decades now. There has never been a need to upgrade again, and doing so just because someone else was buying a bigger home would not have been a good financial decision. It has never felt like a compromise. Staying there, rather than continuing to trade up as our means grew further, has itself been one of the more important financial decisions of our life together.

I have watched this go differently for other people. As income grows, so does the temptation to keep buying a bigger home, a nicer car, each purchase justified by the last raise or the last bonus. I have seen that pattern lead people into exactly the kind of trouble described earlier in this chapter, not through one dramatic mistake, but through a series of upgrades that each seemed reasonable at the time. For most of us, quiet wealth looks like staying in the comfortable home rather than continually trading up. There is no discomfort in that choice, and no unmet ambition sitting behind it. It is simply comfortable, and there has never been a reason to leave it.

This is the question worth sitting with as you think about your own financial life.

Are you building a life that looks successful, or a financial foundation strong enough to support you when no one is watching?

Visible success and financial strength can coexist, but one does not guarantee the other, and the difference often reveals itself only when circumstances force it to.

Lasting wealth is usually built quietly, through ordinary decisions repeated over long periods, without an audience. Its evidence is found not in what others see, but in the freedom it makes possible: peace of mind, flexibility, resilience, and the ability to make choices without financial fear. That is the kind of wealth worth building.

These four chapters, taken together, are the foundation the rest of this book stands on: money as a tool, financial independence as freedom, living below your means as the discipline that funds it, and quiet wealth as the resilience it eventually produces. What comes next are the habits that turn this philosophy into a daily practice, starting with the ones that shaped my own financial life more than any other.

PART TWO

THE HABITS THAT BUILD WEALTH

CHAPTER FIVE

The Habits That Build Financial Security

Financial independence is built through regular acts of attention rather than occasional acts of brilliance. That single idea, more than any specific investment or strategy, explains the difference between people who arrive at financial security and people who do not. It was never the dramatic decision that mattered most in my own life. It was the ordinary one, repeated for decades. Financial security is built one habit at a time. You do not need to master everything in this chapter at once.

The habits in this chapter are not complicated. None required exceptional intelligence, a high income, or perfect timing. They required consistency. No single habit made us financially secure on its own. What did was the combination of many small habits, repeated long enough that they became almost automatic.

For many years, I set aside time to review my financial life, originally every Sunday and later every other week. It was not an elaborate exercise, and it did not consume the day. In those early years, I was still learning how the market worked and what I was actually investing in, the same as anyone starting out, so much of that time went into reading and understanding rather than making changes. I looked at how our investments were performing and considered whether anything needed attention. Some weeks, I did not have the time and let it go. Most weeks, I tried to make the time anyway, because I understood how much that steady, mostly educational habit mattered over the long run.

That review did not involve checking prices every day or reacting emotionally to whatever the market had done that week. The habit was less about watching and more about staying oriented, the way a ship's captain checks a compass, not to change course every hour, but to be certain the course is still correct. That biweekly habit was really the first layer of a broader rhythm. A deeper look at the portfolio itself happened monthly, and a full accounting of where we actually stood, adding up everything we owned against everything we owed, happened quarterly. Each cadence served a different purpose: the frequent reading kept me informed, the monthly review kept the portfolio itself on track, and the quarterly reconciliation told me whether we were actually getting ahead.

In the early years, that habit came with a second one: learning. I did not simply place money into funds because someone told me to. I wanted to understand what I actually owned. I studied how the funds I invested in were structured, what sectors they favored, how much exposure they had to technology, healthcare, consumer goods, and companies overseas. Over the years, my allocation leaned more heavily toward technology than any other sector. This was a personal, intentional decision on my part, not a model for anyone reading this to copy. The lesson is not to imitate my allocation. It is to understand what you own well enough that your allocation, whatever it is, is a choice rather than something that simply happened to you.

That reading habit was not passive. Over the years, it led to real, if modest, adjustments. An article on the case for simple, broad index investing, like the S&P 500, reinforced my confidence in staying the course with that part of my portfolio rather than chasing something more complicated. A different stretch of reading on trends in the energy sector led me to reduce my exposure there before conditions worsened further. And articles on the importance of diversification prompted me to adjust how much exposure I carried in foreign investments. None of these were dramatic moves. They were the kind of small, informed tweaks that the habit itself was designed to produce, evidence that the time spent reading was not just educational in the abstract, but genuinely shaped decisions over time.

Learning is only valuable if it eventually changes behavior. Over time, that understanding shaped the practical decisions we made every month, beginning with how we directed every new dollar we earned. Perhaps the habit I would most encourage every reader to adopt is this one: never leave free money on the table. Throughout my career, I made certain to contribute enough to receive my full employer match before directing money anywhere else. Every plan is different. Some employers match a portion of every dollar you contribute up to a certain percentage of your salary. Others match dollar for dollar. It is also worth understanding your plan's vesting schedule, since some employers require you to remain with the company for a certain period before matched contributions fully belong to you. The specific formula and vesting rules do not matter nearly as much as the principle behind them: find out exactly what your employer offers, on both fronts, and contribute at least enough to capture the full match before you put money anywhere else. Capturing the match should generally come before most other savings goals, though I want to acknowledge an exception worth naming: if you are carrying high-interest debt or have no emergency fund at all, addressing that basic stability may reasonably come first, even ahead of the match, depending on your circumstances. Whenever possible, automate good financial decisions. Automatic contributions remove emotion and make consistency far easier than relying on willpower every month.

Beyond the match, I followed a general order each year that served me well, though this is guidance shaped by judgment, not a fixed rule everyone should follow without question. My employer offered what is technically called a 403(b) plan, functionally similar to the more familiar 401(k), so I will refer to it as a 401(k) here for simplicity. After the match, my next priority was a Roth IRA, in the years my income qualified me to contribute to one, because it offered tax-free growth and greater flexibility than my employer plan. Roth eligibility and contribution rules change over time and depend on your income, so evaluate the best order for you against your own current tax situation rather than assuming it from mine. From there, I worked toward maxing out my 401(k) contributions. My wife worked part time after her company closed and no longer had access to an employer pension or savings plan. That is when I began contributing to a spousal IRA on her behalf, subject to the applicable IRS eligibility rules, rather than leave those years without retirement savings for her.

Not every advisor would order those middle steps exactly the way I did. Some would prioritize maxing out both spouses' IRAs before adding extra contributions to a 401(k) beyond the match, particularly if that plan's investment options are limited. And for some readers, an HSA or paying down high-interest debt should come before any of these later steps. There is no single sequence that fits everyone. What matters is understanding what is available to you, in roughly what order it tends to benefit most people, and applying judgment to your own circumstances rather than following anyone's order, including mine, automatically.

I will also say plainly that I am not going to walk through specific contribution limits or income thresholds in this book. Those figures change nearly every year, and a number that is accurate today will be outdated by the time you are reading this. Whatever the current limits are, look them up through the IRS or a trusted financial resource before you act. The principle that outlasts all of those changing numbers is this: understand what is available to you, claim the full match whenever circumstances allow, and think deliberately about the order of everything that follows.

Each raise brought a related decision, one that repeated itself throughout my career. Every raise should improve your future before it expands your lifestyle. That is one of the quiet behaviors that separates people who become financially independent from people who simply earn more money without ever getting ahead. The habit is easy to state and genuinely difficult to hold to, particularly as income grows and the temptation to expand spending grows right alongside it, but it is one of the most consequential habits in this entire book. Lifestyle inflation is subtle because it rarely arrives all at once. It comes a little at a time, and none of it feels significant by itself. The discipline is not about refusing every upgrade, only about making sure your future benefits first.

I made it a rule never to carry credit card debt. Credit card interest rates are among the highest a consumer will ever pay, and no investment I could reasonably expect to earn consistently would justify carrying that kind of debt from month to month. As a principle, it comes down to this: pay your balance in full whenever possible, and if you are already carrying a balance, focus on a disciplined payoff plan rather than adding new charges on top of it. That rule has nothing to do with what rates happen to be in any given year. It holds regardless of whether the rate is eighteen percent, twenty-three percent, or something different by the time you are reading this.

Our mortgage was a different calculation, and I think it is worth explaining honestly as one strategy that worked for us, not a universal recommendation, because whether to pay down a mortgage aggressively depends on the interest rate, the returns available elsewhere, and your own priorities. My mortgage carried a relatively low rate, so for years I prioritized retirement savings and other investments ahead of extra mortgage payments. Once those goals were fully funded, I began directing additional money toward paying off the mortgage. Had my mortgage carried a much higher rate, I likely would have accelerated those payments much sooner. The lesson has nothing to do with which choice to make. It has to do with letting the math of your own situation decide, rather than a rule borrowed from someone else's.

There was one more savings vehicle in our regular rotation, alongside retirement accounts: a New York 529 plan, used to save for our children's education. Contributions to a 529 plan in New York offer a state tax deduction up to a certain limit, the investments grow tax-deferred, and withdrawals are tax-free when used for qualified education expenses. The broader principle here matters more than the specific plan: plan early for predictable future expenses, like education, without sacrificing your own retirement security to do it. I treated those contributions the same way I treated retirement contributions, as a regular, recurring habit rather than something addressed only when a tuition bill arrived. By the time our sons were ready for college, that account had grown steadily for years, without ever requiring a dramatic lump sum or a moment of financial strain. The specific deduction limits and rules governing 529 plans vary by state and change over time, so as with retirement accounts, verify the current rules in your own state rather than relying on figures that may no longer apply by the time you read this.

I also kept a budget, though the word tends to conjure something rigid and unpleasant. A budget should never feel like punishment. It should feel like clarity. The purpose is not to tell you that you cannot spend money. The purpose is to make sure your spending reflects what matters most to you. Mine was closer to a living document than a fixed rule, designed to reflect changing priorities rather than restrict enjoyment. I estimated what we expected to spend over the course of a year, translated that estimate into a monthly expectation, and then reviewed it every quarter to see how the projection compared to reality. When the numbers diverged, I adjusted the plan rather than abandoning it. A well-run business operates exactly this way, and there is no reason a household should be managed any differently.

Numbers become meaningful only when they tell you whether your habits are actually producing results. Alongside that quarterly budget review, I reconciled our full balance sheet every quarter as well, setting our assets against our liabilities. Most people can tell you their income without much thought. Far fewer can tell you their net worth. Income tells you what is coming in. Net worth tells you whether you are actually getting ahead. I have met people with substantial incomes whose net worth barely moved year over year, because everything coming in was matched by everything going out. I have met others with far more modest incomes whose net worth grew steadily, because they paid attention to the number that actually mattered. The quarterly reconciliation was how I made sure I always knew which category I fell into.

Once a month, separate from that quarterly reconciliation, I reviewed the investments themselves, not to react to short-term movement, but to ask whether the portfolio still fit the long-term plan. And periodically, I went a step further and tested the plan itself against different assumptions. Most major financial institutions now offer planning tools that let you model your retirement date, your expected spending, different savings rates, and different portfolio mixes, and project whether you are on pace to reach your goals or falling short. I never viewed those projections as predictions. They were simply tools that helped answer an important question: if I continue doing what I am doing today, where am I likely to end up? This is a far more useful question than wondering whether the market will rise or fall next year. I used tools like these regularly, not because any particular tool was essential, but because the underlying habit was. I regularly tested my assumptions. Financially disciplined people do not wait until retirement to discover whether they have enough. They ask that question years, sometimes decades, in advance, while there is still time to adjust the answer.

None of this meant we stopped living. We took vacations, celebrated birthdays, enjoyed time with family, and created lasting memories. Financial discipline was never about denying ourselves happiness. It existed to increase our freedom and our margin for error, not to create a lifetime of deprivation. It was about making intentional choices so we could enjoy life without sacrificing our future. I have never once regretted the vacations we took, the time spent with family, or the experiences we shared together. Those memories became part of the return on every financial decision we made. Saving was never the destination. Living was.

People sometimes ask which habit mattered most. I honestly cannot answer that question, because each habit reinforced the next. Saving consistently made investing possible. Investing created growth. Avoiding unnecessary debt preserved that growth. Periodic reviews kept the plan on course. Together, those ordinary habits became something far more powerful than any single financial decision ever could.

Looking back over everything I have just described, one thing stands out to me more than any individual habit. None of it was dramatic. I was not day trading. I was not chasing the hottest stock of the moment or trying to predict where the market would move next. Our approach was straightforward. We avoided credit card debt, contributed enough to receive the full employer match, maximized retirement savings for both of us whenever possible, and directed additional money toward paying down our mortgage when it made financial sense. Throughout that process, we continued to enjoy life. Nobody builds financial security out of a few extraordinary decisions. It comes from ordinary ones, repeated consistently over many years.

CHAPTER SIX

The Cost of Debt

Debt is often described in simple terms, as something either good or bad, safe or dangerous. The truth is more useful than that. Debt is a tool, the same way money itself is a tool, and like any tool, its value depends entirely on how it is used and what it is used for. The real question is never simply how much debt you carry. It is whether that debt is building something in your life or quietly draining something from it.

I think of this as the difference between intentional leverage and unchecked drag. Leverage is debt taken on deliberately, for a clear purpose, with a plan for how it will be repaid and what it will produce in return. A mortgage on a home you can genuinely afford is leverage. A loan that finances an education leading to real earning potential is leverage. Drag is different. Drag is debt that accumulates almost without notice, financing a lifestyle rather than a future, carrying a cost that outlives whatever it purchased. The interest on a credit card balance carried month after month is drag. So is a loan taken out simply because the monthly payment sounded manageable, without much thought given to what came after.

One way I have come to think about debt is that every payment you commit to today reduces the number of choices available to you tomorrow. A smaller monthly obligation gives you more flexibility if an unexpected opportunity appears or if life takes an unexpected turn. Financial independence is built as much by preserving options as by increasing income.

The mechanics of that difference are worth understanding clearly, because they explain why debt can be so costly even when it does not feel costly in the moment. Interest can work in both directions. When you invest, compounding can work for you, turning small, consistent contributions into something much larger over time. When you borrow, interest works against you. Depending on the type of debt, unpaid interest may also compound, causing the balance to grow even faster. This is precisely why the same discipline that makes investing so powerful over decades is exactly what makes carrying debt so dangerous over the same stretch of time. The math does not care which direction it is working in.

Debt carries more than a financial cost. For many people, it also carries an emotional one. It can create stress, limit career choices, strain relationships, and make even ordinary financial decisions feel heavier than they should. Eliminating unnecessary debt does more than improve a balance sheet. It often buys peace of mind.

I want to spend some time on an area where this distinction matters more than almost anywhere else: education. Student loan debt gets discussed in absolute terms more often than almost any other kind of debt. Some voices insist it should be avoided entirely, at any cost. I do not believe the answer is that simple, and our own family's experience shaped that view.

My wife and I grew up without many of the things our sons had access to. We were careful not to let that gap become a reason to hand them everything without any responsibility attached to it. The same thinking carried into education and cars. Having them assume some of the cost was part of the lesson, whether the expense was tuition or a car. We bought the car that got them through high school and college. Once they graduated and wanted something newer, that upgrade was on them to buy and pay off themselves.

When our older son chose to attend a private college, it was a deliberate decision, not an impulse, and we had prepared for it. Years earlier, we had established a New York 529 plan and made thoughtful decisions about how that money was saved and invested. It covered the great majority of the cost. But we also chose to have him assume a modest student loan in his own name.

The loan was not necessary because of a financial shortfall. It was about responsibility. We wanted him to understand that education is an investment requiring commitment and that he had a personal stake in the opportunity he had been given. The goal was never to burden him, but to give him a manageable obligation that he would be responsible for repaying.

Our younger son followed a similar path, although the circumstances differed. He began at a private school before transferring to a public city university. We took the same approach with him: a small loan in his own name, carrying the same responsibility and the same lesson. The specific schools and costs differed, but the underlying principle remained the same.

A manageable loan can teach a young adult how interest works, how credit is built, and what it means to fulfill a financial commitment. I believe that personal responsibility helped our sons approach their education with a greater sense of ownership. Not every parent will see it this way, and that is a reasonable place to differ. For us, however, the goal was not debt avoidance at any cost. It was ensuring that any debt taken on served a clear purpose without becoming a burden.

Education deserves the same evaluation as any other major investment. The question is not simply what it costs, but what opportunities it is likely to create. Borrowing should be weighed against expected earning potential, graduation prospects, and realistic repayment expectations.

A small loan that can reasonably be repaid within a year or two of steady work may teach responsibility without limiting future choices. A loan requiring a decade or more of strained payments is no longer a lesson. It is a genuine financial constraint. That distinction should guide parents based on their child's circumstances rather than on a fixed number.

Some parents may feel guilty asking a child to assume even a small loan when they could afford to cover the entire cost. I would gently push back on that guilt. A modest, manageable loan carried and repaid by the student is not a failure of generosity. It can be a valuable lesson learned through direct experience rather than through advice alone.

We learned that lesson again a few years later, in a different form. We had bought our older son a car to take to school. Later, when he wanted a car of his own, he took out a loan to buy it, and the interest rate on that loan was higher than I would have liked. I was tempted to step in and help him pay it down. My wife rightly talked me out of it. She reminded me that he needed to take responsibility for owning his own car and understand what came with it, high interest rate included. He kept the loan, made the payments, and paid it off entirely on his own. Our younger son, when he wanted a specific car of his own choosing, did the same thing, taking a loan and paying it off himself without either of us stepping in.

Neither loan was ideal on paper. Both carried a higher rate than we would have chosen for ourselves. But the discipline of carrying those loans and paying them off was worth more than the interest they cost. Both of our sons are now doing very well, and I do not think that is a coincidence. Learning to carry a financial obligation and see it through, even an imperfect one, is part of what shapes a young adult into someone who can be trusted with larger responsibilities later. Sometimes the most valuable thing a parent can do is resist the urge to remove a difficulty their child is fully capable of handling.

A car should support your life, not define it. Reliable transportation is important. Impressing other people is not. Cars almost always decline in value, yet many people finance them for years while paying interest on an asset that becomes less valuable every month. That combination deserves careful thought before signing any loan agreement.

Every dollar committed to unnecessary debt is a dollar that cannot be invested, saved, donated, or used to create new opportunities. The true cost of debt extends beyond the interest you pay to include everything that money could have become had it remained working for you instead.

None of this changes the broader caution that runs through this entire book regarding debt in general. Most debt, particularly consumer debt used to finance a lifestyle rather than a future, remains drag rather than leverage, and should be avoided or eliminated as quickly as possible. The interest accumulating against a maxed-out credit card or an auto loan on a vehicle beyond your means offers nothing in return beyond the temporary appearance of a lifestyle you have not actually earned yet. But debt is not a single category, and treating every loan as identically dangerous misses an important distinction.

I have never regretted borrowing thoughtfully for something that improved our family's future. I have, however, seen many people regret borrowing for something they simply wanted a little sooner than they could comfortably afford. Time has reinforced that distinction again and again. The question worth asking, before taking on any debt, is not simply whether you can make the payment. It is whether this debt is building something in your life, or your family's life, that will still be standing long after the debt itself is gone.

That is the real cost of debt, and the real value of debt, held side by side. Debt taken on carelessly drains a future one payment at a time. Debt taken on with intention, in service of something worth building, can do the opposite. The difference is not the presence of debt itself. It is the purpose behind it, and the discipline brought to repaying it.

CHAPTER SEVEN

The Power of Consistent Investing

There is a piece of advice that sounds almost too simple to matter: keep investing, regardless of what the market is doing. I have found, after nearly forty years in the market, that simplicity is exactly what makes it so hard to follow, and exactly why so few people actually do.

Before your money can begin working for you, you first have to remove the habits that continually work against you. This chapter follows the discussion on debt for that reason. Eliminating unnecessary debt creates the capacity to invest consistently, and consistent investing is where long-term wealth is actually built.

In 2008, I watched the same downturn everyone else watched. Financial institutions I had followed for years were suddenly in serious trouble. The market fell sharply, and it kept falling for longer than anyone wanted. Through all of it, I never stopped contributing. My regular contributions continued going in as planned, through the asset allocation I had built over the years, regardless of what the market was doing on any given week. That, more than any single decision I made during that period, is what I would want a reader to take from this chapter. Consistency during a downturn is not a small thing. It is one of the most powerful forces available to a long-term investor, precisely because it is the one thing almost everyone is tempted to abandon at the exact moment it matters most.

It took me years to understand that market declines are often the periods when regular investors make some of their best long-term purchases. When prices fall, every scheduled contribution buys more shares than it did before. It rarely feels rewarding in the moment, because headlines are filled with uncertainty, but years later those purchases often become some of the most valuable investments in the portfolio.

I did not, however, sit entirely still during 2008. As part of the review habit I described earlier, I read consistently about what was happening across the market and within specific industries, and over the years that habit built a real understanding of trends, developed slowly, through repetition, not through any single insight. During the 2008 downturn, that reading told me enough to make some adjustments. I shifted a portion of my portfolio into cash and into mutual funds with less volatility, moving away from some of the financial institutions that concerned me most at the time. The precise scope of that adjustment matters, because it is easy to overstate. It touched roughly a quarter to a third of my overall portfolio, not the whole of it. The rest stayed invested and kept receiving contributions exactly as before.

Readers should not misunderstand what I was doing here. I was not attempting to move my entire portfolio in and out of the market or predict the exact bottom. There was an element of tactical judgment in what I did, and I recognize that such decisions can easily go wrong. The important distinction was that the adjustments affected only part of the portfolio, remained within my broader risk plan, and never interrupted my regular long-term contributions.

I did not time those adjustments perfectly. I moved money out of certain positions before the bottom, and I moved money back in gradually as the market kept falling further, which meant I was buying before it was finished falling as well. There is nothing unusual in that. Nobody, myself included, reliably hits the exact top or the exact bottom. What mattered was not precision. What mattered was that the adjustments were modest, informed by genuine research rather than fear, and that the great majority of my portfolio remained untouched and continued growing through regular contributions the entire time.

Eventually, the broad market recovered, as it had after earlier major downturns during my investing years. That does not mean every company or individual investment recovered. Some financial institutions failed, and others never returned to their previous strength. That experience reinforced the importance of diversification and of not allowing the future of an entire portfolio to depend on any single company or sector.

One reason automatic investing is so effective is that it removes emotion from the process. Contributions continue whether the news is optimistic or pessimistic, reducing the temptation to wait for the perfect time to invest. Over many years, consistency has proven far more valuable than perfect timing.

I make adjustments like that only occasionally, perhaps once or twice a year at most, and always based on trends I have read about and understood over time, not on headlines or a single piece of news. I did something similar with the energy holdings mentioned in an earlier chapter, trimming that exposure in the same modest way as oil prices declined steadily. These are not frequent moves, and something important is worth stating plainly: I am not suggesting the average reader should attempt this kind of tactical adjustment. It comes from years of reading market trends consistently, week after week, and even with that much experience behind it, I still do not get the timing exactly right. What I am recommending, without hesitation, to any reader regardless of experience, is the part that requires no market expertise at all: continue investing through the downturns rather than stopping. If anything, a downturn is exactly when consistent, long-term asset allocation makes the most sense, because you are acquiring more for every dollar contributed than you were before prices fell.

Diversification matters here as well, although my own portfolio was more concentrated than what would be appropriate for many investors. I weighted my investments heavily toward technology because I loved reading about these innovative companies. I was genuinely fascinated by them, and that fascination, more than any formal analysis, is what kept me following the sector so closely. At various points, technology represented somewhere between thirty and forty percent of my portfolio. That concentration increased both my potential return and my potential loss, and it should not be mistaken for broad diversification. Knowing what I know now, I probably would not have stayed that overweight in a single sector for as long as I did. It worked out better than I had any right to expect and grew into a far larger part of my portfolio than I had anticipated, but I would not advise anyone to be that concentrated in one area. I got lucky as much as I got it right.

I reviewed that exposure annually and reduced it when it moved beyond the level of risk I was prepared to accept.

Rebalancing is a disciplined way of bringing a portfolio back toward its intended allocation after market performance causes one area to become disproportionately large. No forecast of the future is required, or attempted. For most readers, a much broader balance across sectors, asset classes, and potentially geographic regions will provide greater protection than the concentrated approach I personally chose.

I have known people over the years who tried to time the market outright, jumping in and out based on predictions about where prices were headed next. Some of them made money doing it, for a while. Almost all of them, over a long enough period, gave a meaningful portion of it back. I am not a financial advisor, and I am not offering this as formal advice. I am simply speaking from what I have observed. Before deciding how aggressively to invest, I believe the more important questions are these: What is your actual goal? What is this money for, and when will you need it? And how much risk are you willing to accept, understanding that greater potential return always comes paired with greater potential loss? For me, this money was my retirement, so I looked closely at the instruments I invested in, understanding that past performance, however carefully back-tested, is never a guarantee of future results. Broad technology indexes and funds have experienced years of gains exceeding twenty-five or thirty percent, as well as years of losses of comparable or greater magnitude. The exact result depends on the index, fund, time period, and investments included. That volatility was the price of pursuing greater long-term growth, and it was a risk I had to be prepared to accept. That is why, when any single position, including my technology holdings, grew beyond the range I was comfortable with, I trimmed it back, regardless of how well it happened to be performing at the time.

I have also encountered people who offer investment advice with great confidence, often because one particular trade worked well for them. I have never taken that kind of advice. I go with my own research and my own understanding, regardless of how loud the noise around a hot stock happens to be. And when my own judgment has been wrong, which it certainly has been at times, that has been acceptable to me, because I am building toward a long horizon, not a single quarter or a single trade. A reader does not need decades of experience reading market trends to succeed with this approach either. Some of the simplest, most accessible investments available, such as an S&P 500 index fund or another well-diversified index fund, have a long, well-documented history of solid long-term performance without requiring any of the tactical adjustments I described earlier in this chapter.

You do not need to limit yourself to the S&P 500 to apply this principle. Broad, low-cost index funds such as the Vanguard Total Stock Market ETF, known by its ticker VTI, have historically produced strong long-term results while providing exposure to a wide range of United States companies. Its precise average return changes depending on the ending date, which is another reason historical figures are evidence of the past rather than a promise about the future. Value-oriented funds, such as the Vanguard Value ETF, known as VTV, provide diversified exposure within the value segment of the United States stock market. They can complement a broader portfolio, but they are not substitutes for a total-market fund because they intentionally emphasize one investment style. These are examples rather than recommendations for every investor. The appropriate investment mix should always reflect an individual's goals, time horizon, and willingness to accept market fluctuations. None of this needs to be complicated. If the idea of researching individual companies or timing sectors feels overwhelming, or you simply do not have the time for it, a broad, diversified fund and a consistent contribution schedule can do the work for you.

Based on my own records and the mix of funds I held, my long-term average return has been strong, though the precise result varies depending on the period measured. That variation illustrates the same lesson about historical performance discussed later in this book. What mattered more than any single average was that the portfolio was diversified, funded consistently, and held through both good years and bad. Its success never depended on achieving a specific return, and my results should not be interpreted as what another investor should expect.

Consistency also depends on not investing money that may be needed in the near future. An emergency reserve and a clear time horizon make it easier to remain invested during a downturn rather than being forced to sell at an unfavorable time. Stocks can decline sharply, and money needed for short-term expenses generally should not depend on the market recovering on a particular schedule.

Investing rewards patience far more often than activity. Some years produce exceptional returns, while others are disappointing. Judging a long-term investment plan by a single year is much like judging a book after reading only one chapter. The real story is revealed only after enough time has passed for compounding to do its work.

After nearly four decades of investing, the lesson I value most has nothing to do with identifying the perfect investment. It is having built a process I could continue through good markets and bad ones alike. A good investment strategy should be strong enough to survive periods when your emotions tell you to abandon it.

That, in the end, is the real power of consistent investing. It is not about outsmarting the market during a downturn, and for the great majority of investors, it should not involve trying to. It is about deciding on a sound, diversified allocation and continuing to contribute to it without interruption regardless of what the headlines say in any given month. For most long-term investors, a disciplined process of diversification, regular contributions, periodic rebalancing, and staying invested offers a more dependable path than repeatedly attempting to predict the market's next move.

CHAPTER EIGHT

Time, Your Greatest Financial Asset

Of everything discussed in this book so far, the habits, the discipline around debt, the consistency required to stay invested through good years and bad, none of it matters as much as the one factor most people give the least thought to when they are young: time. You may be able to earn more income, adjust a budget, restructure a loan, or change a spending habit. But you cannot go back and start ten years earlier than you actually did.

Let me show you what that difference can look like in numbers, because the scale of it tends to surprise people. Most people do not save in neat monthly amounts. They save the way a paycheck actually arrives, every two weeks. Imagine two individuals, each contributing two hundred dollars from every biweekly paycheck to a diversified portfolio, earning a hypothetical eight percent annual return, compounded biweekly. The first begins at age twenty-five and continues until age sixty-five, contributing for forty years and investing a total of two hundred eight thousand dollars. The second begins at age thirty-five and continues until age sixty-five, contributing for thirty years and investing a total of one hundred fifty-six thousand dollars.

Under those simplified assumptions, the person who began at age twenty-five would accumulate just over one and a half million dollars. The person who waited until age thirty-five would accumulate approximately six hundred fifty thousand dollars. The first person contributed only fifty-two thousand dollars more, yet finished with nearly eight hundred seventy-five thousand dollars more, simply because those earlier contributions had an additional decade to compound. The calculation also assumes that all earnings and distributions remain invested throughout the entire period.

These figures are illustrations, not predictions. Real investment returns do not arrive evenly, and actual results will be affected by market performance, investment expenses, taxes, and the timing of contributions. The assumed rate is not a promise of what any particular investment will earn. The lesson is not the precise ending balance. It is that money invested earlier has more time to generate earnings, and those earnings have more time to generate earnings of their own.

The future balances in an illustration like this are stated in future dollars. Inflation will reduce what those dollars can purchase decades from now. That does not weaken the lesson about starting early, but it does mean that retirement goals need periodic review, and contribution amounts should generally rise as income and living costs increase.

Time can improve an investor's ability to recover from market declines, but it does not make investing risk-free. A long time horizon does not guarantee a positive result, and even diversified portfolios can experience extended periods of disappointing performance. Time works best when it is combined with diversification, reasonable costs, an appropriate level of risk, and the discipline to remain invested.

I started later than the person in that example did. I began investing seriously in 1987, several years into my career, not immediately out of school, but earlier than many people do. What pushed me to start when I did was a conversation that came out of nowhere. A colleague with real investing experience mentioned, almost in passing, the importance of asset allocation and consistent investing, even in small amounts. It was not a lecture. It was not something he set out to teach me. He simply said that he had been doing it for years, something he had learned from his own father, and he happened to retire comfortably in his late fifties. Because he was speaking from genuine knowledge and experience, his words carried more weight than most advice. I had already been reading and trying to understand the stock market and various financial instruments on my own, so the conversation came at exactly the right moment. I asked him a lot of questions, and I started contributing to my employer's retirement plan and applying what I learned, consistently, from that point forward. That habit, sustained over the two years that followed, is part of what gave me the financial footing to accept a lower-paying position in 1989, the decision described earlier. That combination, starting reasonably early and never stopping, is a meaningful part of why I was able to leave corporate life comfortably at sixty-one.

I share that not to suggest that late twenties is somehow the ideal starting point, but to make an important point in the other direction. It is never too late to start. Whether you are beginning at twenty-five, thirty-five, or considerably later, the principle remains the same. Someone who begins later may need to save more, work longer, spend less in retirement, or accept a different balance between growth and security. Those are real trade-offs, but they are not reasons to give up. Starting today still creates more opportunity than waiting another year, because the ideal starting date has already passed. It does not matter whether you can contribute a hundred dollars a month, two hundred, or considerably more. What matters is starting, and then maintaining that contribution consistently over time. Once you actually watch a modest, steady contribution begin to grow, year after year, the growth itself becomes encouraging in a way that no amount of advice can replicate on its own. Seeing it happen changes how seriously you take it.

Starting early matters, but so does increasing what you invest as your circumstances improve. A contribution that begins modestly does not have to remain modest forever. Directing part of each raise toward retirement savings allows the investment habit to grow without requiring a dramatic change in lifestyle. Time provides the foundation, but increasing contributions can strengthen the result considerably.

I have also seen the opposite pattern, and it troubles me every time I see it. I have known family members and people close to me who stay entirely clear of the stock market, convinced it is nothing but a gamble, and who therefore never give time the chance to work in their favor at all. I have known others who did invest, but who got in during a moment of excitement, looking for a quick return rather than approaching it with a real time horizon in mind. When the market declined or became more volatile, they became nervous and pulled everything out, sometimes after prices had already fallen substantially, and many of them never returned.

When we are young, we tend to believe we have plenty of time ahead of us, and often we do not, or not as much as we think. The example above shows exactly why: the extra decade, not the extra money, produced most of the difference. That lesson matters more than any specific number. It also means staying consistent and removing emotion from the process. Markets move up and down. Some declines are part of the normal cycle, and others are unexpected shocks. We have lived through both, 2008 and the September 11 attacks among them, and the broad United States market recovered in time after each. Small, consistent investments held over a long enough period allow compounding to do real work, and that is what eventually gives you the freedom to choose. The people I have seen struggle most were usually looking for a quick return, could not separate emotion from what was happening, took on too much risk, failed to diversify, or simply waited too long to start.

A decline in a broadly diversified portfolio may become a realized loss when an investor sells during the downturn. The long-term damage can become even greater when the investor then remains in cash and misses part or all of the eventual market recovery. Reentering is emotionally difficult because the news rarely becomes reassuring before prices have already begun rising. This is why a written plan and automatic contributions can be so valuable. They reduce the number of decisions fear is allowed to make. Selling during a downturn and then remaining in cash, more than almost any other mistake I have observed over nearly four decades, is what costs people the most. It is not because the market failed them, but because they abandoned the one advantage working in their favor: time.

Investment returns have their greatest opportunity to compound when dividends, distributions, and other earnings remain invested. Money repeatedly withdrawn from the portfolio no longer has the same opportunity to participate in future growth.

Time is powerful, but only when money is allowed to remain at work.

That is why this chapter matters more than any single tactic discussed anywhere else. A modest amount, invested consistently and allowed to compound over many years, has the potential to grow into something substantial without requiring constant trading or market prediction. The habits from earlier chapters, living below your means, avoiding unnecessary debt, investing consistently rather than chasing returns, all of them work in service of this one underlying force. Time allows compounding to do much of the work, but only when it is supported by regular contributions, diversification, reasonable costs, and the discipline to remain invested. Your responsibility is to give the process as many years as possible and avoid interrupting it unnecessarily.

The best time to begin may have been years ago, but that date is no longer available. The only date you can act on is today. Begin with what you can afford, increase it when you can, and give the process the one ingredient no investment can manufacture later: time.

PART THREE

PROTECTING YOUR FINANCIAL FUTURE

CHAPTER NINE

Health Is Part of Wealth

Most books about financial planning treat health as a separate subject, something to think about at the doctor's office rather than at the kitchen table where the budget gets reviewed. I have never seen it that way. Health is part of wealth, in two very different senses, and both of them deserve serious attention in a chapter of their own.

The first sense is the most direct. Healthcare is expensive, and it tends to become far more expensive in retirement than most people expect. According to Fidelity's annual Retiree Health Care Cost Estimate, a sixty-five-year-old retiring in 2026 may need approximately $185,500 in after-tax savings to cover healthcare and medical expenses throughout retirement. The estimate assumes enrollment in Original Medicare, Parts A and B, together with Medicare Part D, and includes premiums, deductibles, copayments, prescription costs, and other out-of-pocket expenses. Just as important, it does not include the potential cost of long-term care. That number surprises many people who have not examined the issue closely, but it should not be discovered as an unpleasant surprise somewhere in their seventies. Healthcare needs to be built into retirement planning from the beginning.

This cost catches people off guard for a reason. Medicare, when it becomes available at sixty-five, is genuinely valuable, but it was never designed to cover everything. Premiums, deductibles, copayments, and prescription costs all continue well past the point where many people assume their healthcare expenses are largely behind them. Drug costs in particular have continued to climb, and while there has been some effort at the federal level to address that through subsidies and negotiated pricing, the relief available varies considerably by circumstance, and retirees should plan as though those costs will keep rising rather than assuming help is on the way.

There is also a real decision to make about the type of coverage you choose once you become eligible for Medicare, and I want to address it honestly without pretending I can settle it for you in a few paragraphs. Broadly, you are choosing between Original Medicare, often paired with a Medigap policy and separate prescription-drug coverage, or a Medicare Advantage plan that provides coverage through a private insurer.

One feature of that choice deserves particular attention. Federal law provides a one-time, six-month Medigap open enrollment window beginning when you are both sixty-five or older and enrolled in Part B, during which an insurer generally cannot deny you a policy or charge more because of your health. After it closes, insurers in most states may apply medical underwriting, which can make an initial choice of Medicare Advantage difficult to reverse. Some states provide broader protections, and limited federal rights apply in certain situations, so confirm the rules in your state.

Each approach has advantages and trade-offs, and the right choice depends heavily on your health, the doctors and specialists you want to continue seeing, the prescription drugs you take, and where you live. Entire books have been written about this decision, and I do not intend to replicate them here. What I want you to take from this chapter is simpler: know that the decision exists, understand that it is not one-size-fits-all, and give it the same careful evaluation you would give any other major financial decision. Begin well before you turn sixty-five, not in the weeks immediately before enrollment.

One of the least expensive forms of healthcare is prevention. Regular physical examinations, recommended screenings, vaccinations, dental care, vision care, and addressing small problems before they become larger ones can improve quality of life and, in many cases, reduce the likelihood of more costly treatment later. Prevention is rarely dramatic, but it is often one of the highest-return investments we can make in our future health.

One of the largest gaps in retirement planning is long-term care. Many people assume that Medicare will pay if they eventually need ongoing help at home, in an assisted living facility, or in a nursing home. In most cases, it will not. Medicare may cover limited skilled nursing or rehabilitation services when specific medical requirements are met, but it generally does not pay for extended custodial care, such as ongoing help with bathing, dressing, eating, or other activities of daily living. Those services may be needed at home, in the community, in assisted living, or in a nursing facility.

For many families, the available choices are to pay privately, purchase long-term-care insurance, or qualify for Medicaid under the rules of their state. Medicaid is a major source of long-term-care funding, but eligibility is subject to financial and other requirements. Asset transfers may also be examined under a five-year lookback rule when a person applies for certain long-term-care benefits. This is not an area to begin thinking about only after care is needed.

Long-term-care insurance is one possible planning tool, but it is generally easier to consider while you are younger and still healthy enough to qualify. The cost of coverage is affected partly by the age at which it is purchased, and most individual policies require medical underwriting. A person with significant health conditions may face higher premiums, limited coverage, or may not qualify at all. I have known people who waited until their sixties to look into long-term-care coverage, only to find that a health change in the meantime had already narrowed their options or raised the cost significantly. The lesson is the same either way: this is not a decision to postpone until it becomes urgent.

Long-term care affects more than the person receiving it. It often places significant emotional, physical, and financial demands on spouses, adult children, and other caregivers. Planning ahead protects more than your own finances. It can reduce the burden placed on the people you love during what may already be a difficult time.

Preparing for future healthcare also means making important decisions while you are still able to do so. Documents such as a healthcare proxy, durable power of attorney, living will, and other advance directives can help ensure that your wishes are understood if you are ever unable to communicate them yourself. Review these documents periodically and discuss them with the people who may one day need to act on your behalf.

Insurance will not be the right answer for everyone. Some people may choose to reserve savings or other assets for future care. Others may examine traditional insurance, hybrid policies, family support, or legal and Medicaid planning with qualified professionals. The specific solution will differ from one household to another. What should not differ is the need to acknowledge the risk. A retirement plan that accounts for medical expenses but ignores the possibility of long-term care may be leaving one of its largest financial exposures unaddressed.

All of this is the financial argument for treating health as part of wealth. Rising costs, an aging population, and a healthcare system that is, by most accounts, increasingly stretched all mean your retirement portfolio needs to be large enough to weather expenses that continue climbing for the rest of your life. That is reason enough, on its own, to take this seriously. But I do not think it is the most important reason.

The second sense in which health is part of wealth has nothing to do with a spreadsheet. No amount of financial security can buy back your health once it is seriously compromised, and no portfolio, however large, is worth much if you are not well enough to enjoy what it was meant to provide. There is no guarantee in this area. Genetics, circumstance, and plain bad luck all play a role that no amount of discipline can fully control. But history has shown, again and again, that people who take care of their health, who eat well, who stay active, who address problems early rather than ignoring them, tend to have a meaningfully better quality of life as they age than those who do not.

Good health also protects financial independence in ways that are easy to overlook. Remaining active and independent for longer may reduce medical expenses, delay or lessen the need for assistance, and preserve more choices about how and where you live. Caring for your health is therefore not only a personal investment but also an important financial one.

I have watched serious illness and premature death affect people I knew, and not always gently. I had a friend who died of a heart attack at sixty-one, a few years after retiring in his late fifties. His death reminded me how quickly the opportunity to enjoy what we have built can disappear. I have also known people whose health and independence declined after they became less active. Watching what you eat, staying active, exercising regularly, and receiving appropriate medical care protect something specific: the freedom your savings were meant to buy. Lose your health, and that freedom goes with it, no matter how much you saved.

I think of health, in some ways, the same way I think of the financial habits described earlier. It rewards consistency far more than intensity. A single ambitious effort rarely produces lasting results, in health or in finance. What produces results, over years and decades, is showing up consistently, paying attention, and making the kind of ordinary, unglamorous decisions, about diet, activity, and preventive care, that compound quietly over time, the same way a modest, steady investment does. Neither guarantees an outcome. Both improve the odds considerably.

Physical health is only part of the picture. Mental and emotional well-being deserve the same attention. Strong relationships, meaningful activities, lifelong learning, adequate sleep, stress management, and maintaining a sense of purpose all contribute to a healthier and more fulfilling life. Financial security becomes far more valuable when it supports both physical and emotional well-being.

There is another side to the comparison that deserves attention. A financial portfolio can grow gradually through compounding, but health can move gradually in the opposite direction when it is consistently neglected. The change may be so slow that it is barely noticeable from one year to the next. Poor eating habits, inactivity, missed examinations, unmanaged stress, and health problems left unaddressed can accumulate until the consequences become much harder to reverse.

The encouraging news is that positive habits can compound as well. Small improvements in nutrition, regular physical activity, strength and balance exercises, adequate sleep, and routine preventive care may seem insignificant on any single day, but over many years they can meaningfully improve health, independence, and quality of life.

We may spend decades saving and investing in the hope that one day we will have the freedom to enjoy what we have built. At the same time, if we neglect the body that must carry us into those years, the two investments may be moving in opposite directions. Our financial resources may be growing while our ability to enjoy them is slowly diminishing.

None of this means that eating well, exercising, and receiving preventive care will guarantee lifelong health. Aging is inevitable. Illness can occur despite our best efforts, and none of us knows how long we will live or how life will ultimately end. The goal is to improve the odds of reaching later life with greater strength, mobility, independence, and quality of life. How we care for ourselves over the years cannot control every outcome, but it can meaningfully influence the condition in which we arrive.

If financial independence is about building the freedom to make choices aligned with your values, health is what allows you to use that freedom once you have it. A large portfolio paired with a body that can no longer travel, play with grandchildren, or simply enjoy an ordinary morning is a partial victory at best. Planning for healthcare expenses, preparing for the possibility of long-term care, and caring for your health throughout the years are not separate projects. They are parts of the same plan, approached from different directions.

We cannot control every illness, prevent aging, or know how long we will live. What we can do is improve the odds. We can build financial resources for the care we may need, make thoughtful decisions before our choices become limited, and treat our health with the same patience and consistency we bring to investing. Wealth means having enough money to support your life and the greatest possible opportunity to remain well enough to enjoy it.

If I were advising anyone beginning a financial plan today, I would tell them to build a health plan alongside it. Save for retirement. Invest consistently. But also protect the body and mind that will carry you into those retirement years. The two plans are not competitors. They are partners, and each becomes more valuable because of the other.

CHAPTER TEN

Building an Emergency Fund

Long-term care is a risk that may develop over decades. An emergency fund exists for something else entirely: the unexpected event that arrives tomorrow. A car breaks down. A roof leaks. A medical bill arrives without warning. A job disappears. A family emergency pulls you away with no notice at all. None of these events are unusual. What determines whether they become a minor inconvenience or a genuine financial crisis is almost always the same thing: whether you have money set aside and readily available before it is needed.

Financial advisors commonly recommend keeping three to six months of essential living expenses in an emergency fund, and some guidance, including from the FDIC, leans toward the higher end of that range. As a starting point, that is reasonable. But I have never viewed an emergency fund as a number to reach and then forget. I viewed it as a source of stability, and the right amount depends heavily on your own circumstances. Depending on your age, job security, health, family responsibilities, household income structure, and whether you are still working or already retired, you may decide that more than six months is appropriate. Some households with highly stable income and other reliable resources may be comfortable with less. Households relying on one income, self-employed individuals, and people whose earnings fluctuate may reasonably need a larger reserve, because replacing lost income may take longer and monthly cash flow may be less predictable. But any backup involving credit, which I will discuss shortly, is a second layer of protection rather than an equal substitute for cash already in hand.

It is worth being precise about what "three to six months of expenses" actually means, because the number is easy to miscalculate. I would begin with essential expenses rather than your full normal spending: housing and utilities, groceries, insurance, healthcare and prescriptions, transportation, minimum required debt payments, and necessary family obligations. Discretionary spending, such as dining out, vacations, gifts, and subscriptions, generally does not need to be included, since those are the areas most households can reduce quickly if income is interrupted. The purpose of the fund is to keep the household functioning through a disruption, not to preserve every part of its normal lifestyle without adjustment. It is also worth remembering that not every large expense is actually an emergency. A roof that is aging and will eventually need replacing, annual property taxes, routine car maintenance, holiday spending, and known insurance deductibles are foreseeable costs rather than true surprises. They are better handled through separate planned reserves than by repeatedly drawing down the emergency fund itself. An unexpected roof failure caused by a storm or sudden damage, however, may qualify as a genuine emergency.

I want to walk through how my own approach evolved, because it changed significantly over the years, and the reasoning behind those changes is more useful than any single number I could give you.

Early in my career, I kept approximately three months of essential expenses in cash. I did that deliberately, because I did not want to hold substantially more cash than I believed we needed while we were both earning income and our finances were otherwise stable. Money beyond that reserve could remain invested for long-term growth. As an additional layer of protection, I established a home equity line of credit against our house. If an unusually large expense arose and the cash reserve was not enough, the line could have provided short-term access to funds at what was then generally a lower interest rate than a credit card or an unsecured loan. I renewed it several times over the years and, fortunately, never had to use it.

That approach worked for us, but I would not present a home equity line as a substitute for emergency savings, for a simple reason. A line of credit is borrowed money, not money already saved. Its interest rate may change. Borrowing against it puts your home up as collateral. And access is not necessarily guaranteed under every circumstance. A lender may reduce or suspend a line for reasons entirely outside your control, including a significant decline in your home's value or a material change in your financial condition, and those exact conditions often arrive alongside the same recession or job loss that might cause you to need the money in the first place. For those reasons, I viewed the line as a secondary layer of protection rather than the emergency fund itself. The first three months were available in cash, already ours, regardless of what any lender decided. The home equity line was a backup behind that cash, supported by stable earnings, manageable expenses, and our ability to repay anything we borrowed. It was a calculated approach suited to our circumstances at that particular stage of life, not a universal recommendation for every reader.

The same caution applies even more strongly to credit cards. Available credit can disappear, interest rates can be high, and carrying an emergency balance for months or years can turn one unexpected expense into a prolonged financial burden. Credit may help manage timing, but it should not be mistaken for savings.

As I approached retirement, my thinking changed again. Without the same steady employment income behind us, I no longer wanted to rely on a home equity line as part of the plan, so I eliminated it entirely. In its place, I accumulated a cash reserve covering a year or more of expenses, and that reserve served two distinct purposes, not one. Part of it functioned as a traditional emergency fund, available for the same kind of unexpected expenses described throughout this chapter. Part of it functioned as a retirement spending reserve, intended to reduce the likelihood that we would ever be forced to sell long-term investments during an unfavorable market period simply to cover ordinary living costs. Retirement changes both the nature of your income and the consequences of a prolonged disruption, and the reserve I built reflected that shift.

The balance that made sense earlier in my career, a moderate cash reserve supported by steady earnings and an unused line of credit, no longer suited the stage of life we were entering. Every household should reassess its reserve periodically as employment, health, family responsibilities, debt, and retirement income change, rather than settling on one number early on and leaving it untouched for decades. The reserve should also be reviewed as living costs rise. A fund that once covered six months of essential expenses may cover considerably less several years later if housing, insurance, food, healthcare, and transportation costs have increased.

Wherever the money is kept, a few principles should remain steady. Our emergency fund was never invested in the stock market. Its purpose was not maximum growth. Its purpose was certainty. We wanted to know that if life presented an unexpected expense tomorrow, the money would be available immediately, regardless of what the market happened to be doing. Accessibility does not necessarily mean that every dollar must remain in a single checking or savings account. A household with a larger reserve may keep an initial portion available immediately and place another portion in safe, short-term instruments that can be accessed without meaningful loss or delay. The important point is that the structure matches how quickly the money might reasonably be needed.

We kept ours in a straightforward savings account linked to our checking account. Today, you can compare federally insured savings accounts and money market deposit accounts and seek a competitive interest rate, provided the money remains safe, accessible, and free from significant withdrawal restrictions. A money market mutual fund is different from a bank money market deposit account and is not insured by the FDIC, even though it may still be appropriate for some investors who understand the distinction. Federal deposit insurance is subject to coverage limits and account-ownership rules. Households holding unusually large cash balances should confirm that their deposits remain within applicable insurance limits or spread the funds appropriately among insured institutions. The account does not need to be sophisticated, but there is no reason for emergency money to earn substantially less than it reasonably can while still fulfilling its primary purpose.

The fund should also remain clearly separate from everyday spending and from money invested for long-term goals. That separation reduces the temptation to spend it on things you simply want rather than things you genuinely need in the moment.

For someone starting from nothing, the full target may feel overwhelming. It can help to build the reserve in stages: first enough to cover a common unexpected expense, then one month of essential costs, and eventually the larger amount appropriate for the household. Automatic transfers made each payday can turn the goal into a steady habit rather than a one-time financial burden.

Fortunately, we rarely had to draw on it in any significant way. Knowing it was there often mattered more than actually using it. It allowed us to face the ordinary surprises of life, the kind every family eventually faces, without panic and without reaching for a credit card or a loan. That peace of mind, quiet and mostly invisible, was one of the best returns that account ever provided, even though it never once appeared on a performance statement.

Before using the fund, I ask myself whether the expense is necessary, whether it was truly unexpected, and whether it is urgent enough that waiting is not realistic. An expense does not have to meet every one of those conditions perfectly, but thinking it through this way helps distinguish a genuine emergency from an inconvenient or impulsive purchase.

An emergency fund is not finished simply because it has reached its target. If money is withdrawn for a genuine emergency, rebuilding the reserve should become a priority once the immediate crisis has passed. That may require temporarily reducing discretionary spending or slowing additional investing, while still giving careful consideration to contributions needed to receive an available employer match. The fund is meant to be used when necessary, but it must also be restored so that one emergency does not leave the household exposed to the next.

An emergency fund is only one piece of a larger safety net, and it is worth seeing how it fits alongside the others. The emergency fund protects you from short-term surprises. Insurance, which we will discuss in the next chapter, protects you against specific, larger risks. Retirement savings build toward long-term financial independence. Long-term-care planning, discussed in the previous chapter, prepares for a possibility that may not arrive for decades, if it arrives at all. Each piece covers a different stretch of time and a different kind of risk. Cash provides flexibility, but it cannot absorb every major financial loss. Some risks are too large to self-fund comfortably, which is why the next layer of protection is insurance. Together, they form a more resilient answer to a simple, unavoidable question: what happens when life does not go according to plan?

CHAPTER ELEVEN

Insurance, Protecting What You've Built

An emergency fund can absorb the ordinary surprises of life, but as the previous chapter noted, cash cannot absorb every loss. Some risks are simply too large to self-fund comfortably, no matter how disciplined the saving behind them. That is where insurance comes in. Insurance is not an investment. It will never make you wealthy, and it is not designed to. Insurance is a way of transferring certain financial risks that would be difficult or impossible for most families to absorb entirely on their own to an institution designed to share those risks across many policyholders. Understood that way, insurance is a decision rather than a purchase, one to be revisited periodically and built around three simple questions.

The first question is this: what financial risks could my family not absorb on our own? A minor car repair is not one of them. Most households, especially once an emergency fund is in place, can cover that without much disruption. A house burning to the ground is a different matter entirely. So is a lawsuit following a serious accident, an illness or disability that interrupts income for months or years, or the loss of the person whose income the rest of the family depends on. The test is not expense alone, but whether a loss would be large enough, or unpredictable enough, that absorbing it would threaten everything else you have built.

The second question follows naturally: which of those risks should be transferred to an insurance company, and which are better handled through your own savings? As your emergency fund and overall net worth grow, a real shift takes place. Risks that once required insurance can increasingly be absorbed personally, while insurance becomes more narrowly focused on the risks large enough to be genuinely catastrophic. A practical example of this is the deductible on your homeowners or auto policy. Early on, a lower deductible in exchange for a higher premium may make sense, because a large out-of-pocket cost would be difficult to absorb. As your reserves grow, raising that deductible, accepting a bit more personal risk on the small losses in exchange for a lower premium over time, often becomes the smarter choice. A higher deductible is useful only when the household can comfortably pay it at any time. Lower premiums are not a true savings if the deductible would create a financial hardship when a claim occurs. Insurance should exist to protect against the losses that would genuinely hurt, not to eliminate every minor inconvenience along the way.

The third question is the one people neglect most: how do these answers change as life changes? Insurance needs are not fixed. They shift as you marry, buy a home, have children, watch your income grow, build savings, watch your children become financially independent, and eventually retire. A policy that made sense at thirty may be entirely wrong at sixty, not because anything was done incorrectly the first time, but because the underlying risks being protected against have changed.

Homeowners insurance is a clear example of the first question in practice. Our home has always been our largest single asset, and I have never had to use that policy, not once. But knowing it was there, protecting against fire, covered storm damage, liability claims, and other insured property losses, provided a kind of peace of mind that had nothing to do with ever filing a claim. The best outcome is never needing the coverage, but you are grateful it exists on the rare occasion you do. Standard homeowners policies generally do not cover flood or earthquake damage, which may require separate coverage. Homeowners should also understand the difference between market value and replacement cost. The amount a home could sell for is not the same as the cost of rebuilding it after a major loss. Construction costs, labor, materials, debris removal, and local building requirements can make the rebuilding cost significantly different from the home's purchase price or current market value.

Automobile insurance illustrates the same principle, and I have a direct example from our own family. My wife was in an accident in a parking lot, struck on the front left side by another driver who was turning. Because we carried collision coverage and rental reimbursement, our insurer was able to handle the repairs and temporary transportation while responsibility for the accident was being resolved. Our insurance company handled the claim directly, sent the car to a body shop they worked with regularly, and provided a rental car for the entire time the repairs were underway, at no additional cost to us. They later recovered both the repair costs and our deductible from the other driver's insurance company. What could have become a drawn-out dispute, a significant unplanned expense, or weeks without a vehicle, became little more than an inconvenience, largely because the right coverage was already in place before it was needed. Liability coverage, in particular, protects your financial future if you are ever responsible for injuring someone else or damaging their property. Uninsured and underinsured motorist coverage deserves attention as well. It can help protect you when the person who causes an accident has no insurance or does not carry enough coverage to pay for the injuries or losses involved. The adequacy of another driver's insurance is one risk you cannot control after an accident has already occurred.

Disability insurance is, in my view, the most overlooked coverage among working families. Most people insure their home. Most insure their car. Fewer insure their own ability to earn an income, despite the fact that, for most working households, future earning power is the single largest financial asset they have. A serious illness or injury that ends or interrupts your ability to work can undo years of disciplined saving faster than almost anything else. It is worth asking seriously, at any stage of your career, whether that risk is one your family could genuinely absorb without protection. Anyone evaluating disability coverage should look beyond the monthly benefit alone. The definition of disability, the waiting period before benefits begin, the length of time benefits may continue, whether benefits are taxable, and whether the policy protects the ability to work in your own occupation can all materially affect the value of the coverage.

Umbrella liability insurance deserves attention for the same reason. As savings and investments grow, so does what a serious lawsuit could take from you. An umbrella policy extends liability protection beyond the limits of your homeowners and auto coverage, typically at a relatively modest cost given the protection it provides. Many financially secure families carry one for exactly this reason: the more you have built, the more there is to protect, and a single serious liability claim, without adequate coverage, could undo a great deal of that work at once. An umbrella policy generally requires the underlying homeowners and automobile policies to maintain specified liability limits. It is therefore important to review all three together rather than purchasing umbrella coverage in isolation and assuming every claim will automatically be covered.

Life insurance is where the third question, how your needs change over time, applies most clearly in our own experience. While I was working, I carried life insurance provided through my employer, along with a modest additional amount, to make sure our family would be protected if something happened to me while our children were still financially dependent on us. Term insurance served that purpose well during those years. When our children were young and depended on our income, life insurance was an essential part of our financial plan. As our investments grew, our debts declined, and our children became financially independent, our financial assets eventually became the protection that life insurance once provided. For me, the decision was straightforward: I carried life insurance because there was a genuine need for it, and once our sons were grown, working, and earning their own income, that need was gone. Rather than keep paying premiums for protection we no longer needed, I preferred to have that money invested and working in our portfolio. By the time I left corporate life, I no longer felt life insurance was necessary, and I have not carried it since. Other families, depending on their own circumstances, debts, or dependents, may reasonably reach a different conclusion. The need for life insurance should be based on the financial obligations that would remain after death, including income replacement, mortgage or other debts, education costs, final expenses, and support for anyone who is financially dependent on you. The appropriate amount may decline over time, but it deserves review rather than assumption.

Permanent life insurance may serve a purpose in certain estate-planning, business, or lifelong dependent situations, but it is more complex and usually more expensive than term coverage. Buy it to meet a specific need, not simply because it combines insurance with a cash-value feature.

One detail worth flagging for anyone relying on employer-provided life or disability coverage, as I did for years: that protection is often tied to your employment, and it can disappear the moment you change jobs or retire. It is worth knowing exactly what your employer provides, what portion of it ends the day you leave, and whether you would want to replace any of it independently before that coverage lapses. Coverage gaps can be especially dangerous during job changes, retirement, divorce, relocation, or major purchases. Those transitions are natural times to review insurance because the risks may change before replacement coverage is fully in place.

One further habit is worth mentioning: reviewing your coverage periodically, not just deciding once and assuming it still fits years later. Many people insure a home for what they originally paid for it decades ago, rather than what it would actually cost to rebuild today. Vehicles change in value. Home improvements add value that may not be reflected in an old policy. Collectibles and valuables accumulate over the years. Review beneficiary designations after marriage, divorce, births, deaths, and other major family changes. These designations may control who receives the proceeds regardless of what is written in a will, so outdated information can produce consequences the policyholder never intended.

It is also worth remembering that every policy has limits. Deductibles, exclusions, and coverage caps are written into the fine print of every policy you own, and the time to understand them is before you need the coverage, not while you are in the middle of a claim. A few minutes spent reading through what a policy actually excludes can prevent an unpleasant surprise at the worst possible moment. It is also worth knowing whether a policy can be renewed, whether premiums may increase, and whether the insurer has the financial strength to meet future claims. The lowest premium is not always the best value if the coverage is narrow, the exclusions are significant, or the company's claims service is poor.

Self-employed individuals and business owners may face additional risks that employees do not, including business interruption, professional liability, key-person loss, and the loss of income during an extended disability. Their insurance review should include both household protection and the financial risks created by the business itself.

Insurance cannot prevent tragedy, illness, accidents, or natural disasters. Nothing can. What it can do, when chosen thoughtfully and reviewed periodically, is prevent those events from becoming financial catastrophes on top of everything else. The purpose of insurance was never to make you wealthy. It was always to protect what you have spent years working to build.

Insurance is one of those expenses people sometimes question because they hope they never have to use it. That is precisely the point. The value of insurance is not measured by how often a claim is filed, but by whether the coverage is there when a loss would otherwise threaten years of careful saving and investing. Matched to the risks that truly matter, and revisited as life changes, insurance helps ensure that one unexpected event does not undo the work of decades.

CHAPTER TWELVE

Why Smart People Still Get Money Wrong

Intelligence and financial wisdom are not the same skill, and one of the more humbling truths I have observed over nearly four decades in finance is how often the two fail to travel together. I have known brilliant engineers, respected physicians, and sharp attorneys who could analyze almost any problem in their own field with real precision, and who still made financial decisions that undermined years of hard-earned income. It is tempting to assume that a person capable of mastering a demanding career would naturally be capable of managing money well. In practice, the two require different muscles entirely, and building one does not automatically build the other. But this is not only a story about smart people. It is a story about anyone who assumes there is more time ahead than there actually is, who spends more than they should today in the belief that they will catch up later, only to find that catching up requires far more than they expected once the years have passed.

Much of the reason comes down to something simpler than intelligence: fear of the unknown. Building a strong financial future requires consistency and discipline, sustained over years most people would rather not think about too closely. That kind of long-term commitment can feel uncomfortable, even threatening, to someone who has not taken the time to understand it. Rather than face that discomfort directly, by learning, planning, and committing to a consistent approach, many people avoid the subject altogether, and avoidance quietly becomes its own decision.

Closely related is a tendency to live for today, trusting that things will simply work out. To be fair, for many people, they often do, at least for a while, and that is part of what makes the pattern so persistent. Believing there is plenty of time to start building real financial security is one of the most common and most costly assumptions I have encountered. As we discussed earlier, when it comes to compounding, time given up early is exceptionally difficult to recover later, no matter how much discipline is applied afterward. A decade lost to the belief that there would always be time later is a decade that cannot be purchased back, at any price, once it has passed.

I have also seen people rely on external factors to carry them financially: an inheritance from a parent, a windfall they expect but cannot control, a spouse's career, or a business deal that has not yet materialized. Depending on a factor outside your own control is not a plan. The expected financial support may never materialize, or it may arrive later, in a smaller amount, or under very different circumstances than expected. None of this replaces the discipline of building your own financial foundation, because a plan built on someone else's decisions is not really a plan at all. Financial vulnerability can also attract people who promise certainty, unusually high returns, or opportunities that supposedly carry little risk. Intelligence does not provide immunity from fraud. In some cases, confidence in one's own judgment can make a persuasive story even harder to question.

The same principle applies to income. A high salary can hide weak financial habits for many years, in the same way that lifestyle inflation, which we looked at earlier, can quietly absorb a raise before it ever strengthens savings. As long as enough money continues arriving, overspending, inadequate saving, and the absence of a real plan may not appear urgent. The danger becomes visible only when the income changes, through retirement, illness, job loss, or an unexpected career transition. Earning more provides greater opportunity, but it does not automatically create security. Without disciplined decisions, a larger income can simply support a more expensive version of the same financial vulnerability.

Underneath all of these patterns sits a broader truth that behavioral finance research has documented extensively: poor financial decisions are rarely the result of insufficient intelligence. They are far more often the result of being human. Regardless of education or professional success, people are vulnerable to overconfidence, loss aversion, giving too much weight to recent events, following the crowd, and preferring an immediate reward over a larger benefit that may take years to arrive. A widely cited study of more than sixty-six thousand brokerage households found that the investors who traded most frequently earned substantially lower net returns than less active investors during the period examined. The lesson is not that every investment decision should be avoided. It is that visible activity can easily be mistaken for thoughtful progress, even when costs, taxes, and poor timing are reducing the result. Intelligence does not protect anyone from these tendencies. In some cases, it can make them more dangerous, because a sharp mind is often very skilled at constructing a convincing explanation for what emotion, ego, or impatience has already decided.

Another powerful influence is loss aversion. People often experience the pain of a financial loss more intensely than the satisfaction of an equivalent gain, which can distort decisions during periods of uncertainty. That fear can lead them to hold a failing investment too long because selling would make the loss feel permanent. It can also push them out of a sound long-term investment during a market decline, only to return after prices have recovered. In both cases, the decision is driven less by the underlying plan than by the desire to escape emotional discomfort. I watched this happen to a friend of mine. He was invested in the market, but his attention was on short-term gains, and he was carrying more risk than he understood. When prices began falling, he sold everything, and he sold while they were still falling, which turned a decline on paper into a significant, permanent loss. It took him a long time to come back to the market at all. The broader market eventually recovered, but he did not participate fully in that recovery.

A related mistake is allowing past decisions to control future ones. People sometimes continue holding an unsuitable investment, supporting an unprofitable business, or pouring money into a failing project because they have already invested so much in it. But money already spent cannot be recovered simply by committing more. Financial wisdom requires evaluating a decision based on what makes sense from this point forward, not on how much time, pride, or money has already been invested in the past. This is commonly known as the sunk-cost effect. Recognizing it does not make the decision emotionally easy, but it helps separate what has already been lost from what still has the potential to be protected.

Success can create a different danger: overconfidence. A person who has succeeded through intelligence, judgment, and hard work in one profession may naturally believe those same abilities will transfer directly to investing, tax planning, insurance, or retirement decisions. Sometimes they do. But financial markets do not reward confidence merely because it was earned elsewhere. Knowing when to seek qualified advice, when to admit uncertainty, and when to follow a disciplined plan instead of acting on instinct are forms of financial intelligence in their own right. Accomplishment should create confidence. It should not eliminate curiosity, or the willingness to ask questions outside your own field. Once people become committed to an investment or financial belief, they may also begin seeking information that supports it while dismissing evidence that challenges it. This confirmation bias can make a weak decision feel stronger simply because opposing information is no longer being considered honestly.

Following the crowd creates another form of false reassurance. When everyone around you appears to be buying the same investment, chasing the same opportunity, or adopting the same lifestyle, the decision can feel safer simply because it is widely shared. But popularity does not reduce risk, and agreement does not guarantee wisdom. Some of the most damaging financial decisions are made not in isolation, but in the comfort of knowing that many other people are making them too. It is the same comparison trap explored earlier, now driving investment decisions rather than spending ones. Recent events can distort judgment as well. After a long market rise, people may assume strong returns will continue indefinitely. After a severe decline, they may believe losses will continue forever. In both cases, the most recent experience begins to feel more permanent and more predictive than it really is.

I think of this the same way I think of health, a comparison I have already drawn. When we are young, our bodies absorb almost anything we put them through, and it is easy to believe that pattern will continue indefinitely. We eat what we want, we live the way we want, and for a long stretch of time, nothing seems to go wrong. Slowly, often without any single dramatic moment, the body begins to show the effects of years of neglect, and for some people, by the time the consequences become impossible to ignore, the path is difficult to reverse. Financial habits follow the same quiet trajectory.

One reason these patterns survive for so long is that the consequences are delayed. A poor financial decision does not always produce an immediate crisis. The bills may still be paid. The markets may continue rising. Retirement may still seem distant. That delay creates the illusion that the decision carried no real cost. But financial consequences often accumulate silently before they become visible. By the time the problem finally demands attention, years of potential compounding may already have been lost, debts may have grown, and the range of available choices may have narrowed considerably.

This same pattern shows up in two other places, both of them already discussed. Skipping an emergency fund rarely feels like a mistake while nothing has gone wrong yet. Letting an insurance policy lapse, or never updating one as life changes, rarely feels urgent until the year it matters most. Both are behavioral failures as much as financial ones, postponed not because the reasoning is unclear, but because the cost of postponing is invisible until the exact moment it stops being invisible.

What connects nearly all of these mistakes, including the fear of starting, the belief that time is unlimited, and dependence on outside factors, is a failure to step back and look at the whole financial picture rather than simply reacting to what is directly in front of you today. It is easy to focus entirely on today's paycheck, today's bills, today's immediate pressures. It is much harder, and far more valuable, to periodically ask a different set of questions. Where am I right now, honestly? What are my actual plans for the years ahead? Am I building toward something intentional, or am I simply reacting to whatever this week happens to require? A plan for tomorrow has to be built today, deliberately, because tomorrow has a way of arriving whether or not you were ready for it.

Awareness matters, but awareness alone is not always enough. Good financial behavior becomes easier when important decisions do not have to be made repeatedly in moments of emotion or distraction. Automatic retirement contributions, scheduled transfers to savings, automatic bill payments, a written investment plan, and periodic portfolio reviews, the kind described earlier, can turn good intentions into consistent action. These systems do not eliminate the need for judgment, but they reduce the number of opportunities for fear, procrastination, or impulse to take control.

A written plan is especially valuable during periods of uncertainty. It is easy to promise yourself that you will remain disciplined when markets are calm and income is secure. It is much harder when prices are falling, headlines are frightening, or personal circumstances suddenly change. Deciding in advance how much you will save, how your investments will be allocated, when you will rebalance, and under what circumstances you will make a major change creates a standard against which emotional decisions can be tested. For major financial decisions, creating a deliberate pause can also be valuable. Waiting a day or two before making a large purchase, changing an investment strategy, or acting on an alarming headline gives emotion time to settle and allows the decision to be measured against the written plan.

Financial wisdom also requires humility. No one understands every area of finance equally well, and the cost of pretending otherwise can be substantial. There are times when the right decision is to learn more, times when it is to remain patient, and times when it is to seek help from a qualified professional whose training, compensation, and responsibilities are appropriate to the decision being made. This is not about surrendering responsibility for your financial life. Taking responsibility sometimes includes knowing the limits of your own knowledge.

None of this is a matter of intelligence, and it is not a character flaw exclusive to people who struggle financially. It is a deeply human pattern, one that affects capable and accomplished people as often as anyone else, sometimes more, because success in one area can quietly convince a person that there is less to learn in another.

The advantage available to anyone willing to examine these patterns is awareness followed by action. Once you recognize the fear of starting, the pull of living entirely for today, dependence on factors outside your control, overconfidence, and the temptation to let emotion replace a plan, you are already in a better position to correct course. But recognition must eventually become behavior. Automate what can be automated. Write down the decisions that matter. Review the entire financial picture periodically. Seek help when the limits of your knowledge require it.

Financial wisdom is not about being the smartest person in the room. It is about being honest enough to see where you actually stand, humble enough to keep learning, disciplined enough to follow a sound plan, and consistent enough to act before years of drift make the correction significantly harder.

These twelve chapters form the foundation for everything that follows. We have examined the philosophy behind money, the habits that build financial security, the behavioral mistakes that weaken it, and the protections that preserve it. The chapters ahead turn from accumulation and protection to the decisions involved in living on what you have built, beginning with one of the most consequential choices in retirement: when to claim Social Security.

PART FOUR

MAKING RETIREMENT WORK

CHAPTER THIRTEEN

Understanding Social Security Before You Claim

Few retirement decisions carry as much long-term weight as when to claim Social Security. Once you claim, the reduction from filing early or the increase earned by delaying is generally built into your benefit for life, subject to annual cost-of-living adjustments and the limited exceptions Social Security's rules allow. This is not a choice to make casually, out of habit, or simply because a particular birthday arrives on the calendar.

The basic mechanics are worth understanding first. Full retirement age for anyone born in 1960 or later is sixty-seven. You may claim retirement benefits as early as sixty-two, but for someone whose full retirement age is sixty-seven, doing so reduces the monthly benefit by thirty percent. Delay beyond full retirement age, and your own retirement benefit earns delayed retirement credits of eight percent per year until age seventy, when the credits stop accumulating. For the same earnings record, the benefit at seventy is seventy-seven percent higher than the benefit at sixty-two. Future cost-of-living adjustments are also applied to that larger amount.

Those rules apply to your own retirement benefit. Spousal and survivor benefits work differently, and that is where much of the confusion begins for married couples.

There is no single correct age to claim, despite what generic rules of thumb may suggest. The right timeline depends on your health, other income, plans to continue working, family history of longevity, and, if you are married, how your decision interacts with your spouse's record. None of us knows how long we will live. Delaying benefits is, in many ways, a form of longevity insurance.

My wife and I did not claim at the same age, and we did not use the same strategy. She began taking her own retirement benefit at sixty-five. Based on her earnings history, her benefit was smaller, and given our overall financial picture, the additional dollars she would have received by waiting did not justify giving up the income in the meantime. I am delaying my own benefit until age seventy. Because my benefit base is higher, waiting produces a significantly larger increase in dollar terms.

We reached that decision by looking at both benefit estimates together and asking what each additional year of waiting was actually worth in dollars, and what it would mean for whichever one of us lived longer. That was the right answer for our numbers.

An age-based spousal benefit is calculated using the worker's benefit at full retirement age, formally called the primary insurance amount. If the claiming spouse waits until his or her own full retirement age, the maximum spousal amount is generally fifty percent of the worker's primary insurance amount. If the higher earner delays until seventy and receives a larger check, those delayed retirement credits do not increase the maximum spousal benefit.

A spouse may generally claim an age-based spousal benefit as early as sixty-two, but claiming before full retirement age permanently reduces it. For a spouse whose full retirement age is sixty-seven and who is entitled only on the worker's record, claiming at sixty-two can reduce the amount to 32.5 percent of the worker's primary insurance amount rather than fifty percent. When the spouse also qualifies on his or her own earnings record, the calculation is more complicated because the individual and spousal portions may be reduced separately.

A current spouse generally cannot receive a spousal benefit until the worker has filed. Social Security pays the spouse's own retirement benefit first and then adds any spousal amount necessary to bring the total to the higher applicable benefit. It does not pay two complete benefits. If the spouse's own primary insurance amount equals or exceeds fifty percent of the worker's primary insurance amount, no spousal addition is payable. If the spouse claimed his or her own benefit before full retirement age, that reduction remains. A later spousal addition does not erase it, so the combined amount will generally be less than a full fifty percent.

Another rule closes off a strategy readers may still encounter in older books and articles. For people born on or after January 2, 1954, deemed filing generally applies when they are eligible for both their own retirement benefit and a spousal benefit. Filing for either is treated as filing for both. The former strategy of collecting only a spousal benefit while allowing one's own retirement benefit to grow until seventy is generally no longer available to this group.

Survivor benefits follow a different set of rules. A survivor benefit is not limited to half of the deceased spouse's benefit. An eligible surviving spouse who has reached full retirement age for survivor benefits may generally receive up to one hundred percent of what the deceased spouse was receiving or was entitled to receive, including delayed retirement credits the deceased spouse had earned. Those credits may therefore increase the income available to the survivor after one spouse dies.

This was the second reason delaying made sense in my case. Increasing my own benefit does more than raise the income we can receive later while we are both living. If I die first, it may also strengthen the income floor available to my wife for the rest of her life.

Survivor benefits may generally begin as early as age sixty, or age fifty for someone with a qualifying disability, but claiming before survivor full retirement age permanently reduces the rate. For an age-based claim at sixty, the survivor generally receives about 71.5 percent of the applicable amount, with the percentage increasing toward one hundred percent at survivor full retirement age. Survivors have their own full retirement age, set by the surviving spouse's birth year and falling between sixty-six and sixty-seven. For some birth years it arrives a few months earlier than the age that governs retirement benefits. Waiting past it does not increase the survivor benefit.

If the deceased spouse claimed a reduced retirement benefit before full retirement age, a separate provision may limit what the survivor receives. In general, the limit is the greater of 82.5 percent of the deceased worker's primary insurance amount and the amount the worker would have been entitled to receive if still alive, before any reduction that applies because the survivor claims early.

Social Security does not pay a full retirement benefit and a full survivor benefit at the same time. The total is generally equal to the higher applicable amount. Deemed filing, however, does not apply to survivor benefits in the same way it applies to retirement and spousal benefits. Depending on the circumstances, an eligible survivor may be able to claim one benefit first and switch to the other later if it becomes larger.

Returning to your own benefit, if you claim before full retirement age and continue working, earnings above the annual limit may cause part of your benefit to be temporarily withheld. Those amounts are not permanently lost. At full retirement age, Social Security generally recalculates the monthly benefit to account for the months in which benefits were withheld.

Waiting also requires the financial capacity to wait. If you have retirement savings, a pension, annuity income, taxable investments, or other resources that can comfortably support you before age seventy, using those resources may allow your Social Security benefit to continue growing. If Social Security is needed to meet current living expenses, delaying may not be realistic regardless of how attractive the later number appears.

Social Security should therefore be coordinated with the rest of the retirement income plan: pensions, annuities, retirement-account withdrawals, taxable investments, taxes, and the required minimum distributions that eventually apply to certain accounts. Medicare requires separate attention. Delaying Social Security does not necessarily mean that you should delay Medicare, and failing to enroll on time can create coverage gaps or late-enrollment penalties unless an exception applies. Depending on total income, up to eighty-five percent of Social Security benefits may be included in federally taxable income. Some states tax benefits and many do not.

Individuals who are divorced may have claiming options based on a former spouse's earnings record if the eligibility requirements are met, including, generally, a marriage lasting at least ten years. Different rules and exceptions may also apply in cases involving disability, a child in a spouse's care, or other special circumstances. Those situations are beyond the scope of this chapter but are another reason not to rely on a simplified formula.

Begin reviewing your own estimates, and your spouse's if you are married, several years before you expect to file. Compare the actual dollar amounts at different ages. Review your Social Security earnings statement to make sure your work history and reported earnings are correct. Errors are easier to address years in advance than in the months immediately before filing.

The ages and percentages in this chapter reflect the rules in place as this book goes to press. Congress has changed Social Security before and could do so again. Confirm the current rules and your own eligibility with the Social Security Administration before acting.

Deciding to delay my benefit was one of the more valuable choices we made in planning our retirement income, because it fits our larger plan and strengthens the long-term security of our household. What I want you to take from this chapter is not a particular age to claim. It is the importance of understanding what each choice does, examining both spouses' records together, and treating survivor protection as part of the decision rather than an afterthought.

Social Security is one part of living on what you have built. Its rules may be technical, but its purpose is deeply practical: creating an income stream that supports the life ahead. Once that financial foundation is in place, a larger question begins. What will you do with the freedom it helps provide?

CHAPTER FOURTEEN

Retirement Is Freedom, Not the End of Purpose

When to claim Social Security is a technical decision with an answer specific to your numbers. What retirement itself is for is a much larger question, and a far less technical one. Retirement is one of the most misunderstood words in the English language. Most people think of it as an ending, the day the working years stop and something vaguely called leisure begins. I have come to see it very differently. Retirement is not the end of purpose. It is a shift in the freedom to choose what that purpose looks like next. And what you do with that freedom matters far more than most people realize before they get there.

I have watched two very different versions of retirement play out among people I have known, and the difference between them has stayed with me. Some people retire and treat it as an endgame, in the truest sense of the word. They sell the home, move somewhere warm, and settle into a rhythm built almost entirely around rest and leisure. For some, that genuinely works, at least for a while. For others, without something actively keeping the mind and body engaged, decline can set in far more quickly than anyone expects.

I have already told you about the friend who died at sixty-one, a few years after retiring. That loss stayed with me, and it is part of why I did not want leaving corporate life to mean becoming disengaged. It reminded me to continue giving serious attention to my health, meaningful activity, and daily structure.

My own transition looked very different, though it did not start with any grand plan. I was not doing nothing. I was consulting and managing our investments. But after decades in a role that demanded constant focus, leaving felt good at first, and then, as the months passed, I began to feel a kind of empty space, a quiet doubt about whether I had made the right decision. I enjoy staying busy, and consulting and managing investments alone were not enough to fill that need. It took roughly six months away from the pace I had kept for so long to actually think clearly about what came next, free of the routine I had been locked into for years. That is when I realized I had already spent years writing and jotting down ideas and reflections on books I had read, without ever calling it anything. That recognition is what led me to start writing in earnest, beginning with something for my grandson, and it became the part of this second act that has stuck with me the most. Writing gave me a project, a purpose, and a reason to keep learning and growing, the same way a demanding career once did.

I share that not because writing is the answer for everyone, but because having something, anything, that keeps you engaged is the answer for nearly everyone. It does not need to be a book. It could be teaching, mentoring, volunteering, a serious hobby pursued with real intention, or continued part-time work in a field you actually enjoy. What matters is not the specific activity. What matters is that it keeps you moving, keeps you thinking, and gives your days a sense of direction that retirement, left completely unstructured, does not automatically provide on its own.

For me, one unexpected source of this came through the monthly newsletters I publish. Many of the people who read them, young accountants especially, have reached out for mentorship: how to build credibility with senior leadership early in a career, what a first year as a Corporate Controller actually teaches you, how to build a high-performing team. I built a page on my own website around it, since enough people were asking that it made sense to gather the questions in one place. Some want a conversation. Others simply post a question and want an honest answer. I received mentorship myself when I was starting out, and there is a particular kind of satisfaction in giving that back. It costs very little to offer, and it means more to the person receiving it than most people expect.

Purpose is not only mental. Retirement also offers a genuine opportunity to invest in physical health, through regular exercise, walking, strength training, and healthy habits. Staying physically active supports independence, reduces the risk of chronic illness, and complements the mental and social engagement that the rest of this chapter focuses on. The two work together, not separately.

Many people also underestimate how much structure a career provides. The routine of waking with a purpose, interacting with others, solving problems, and working toward meaningful goals can disappear almost overnight once a career ends. Retirement often requires more than a financial adjustment. It requires an adjustment in identity. For many people, a career becomes closely connected to how they see themselves and how others see them. When that role ends, it is natural to ask, "Who am I now?" The healthiest transitions often come from replacing that identity with new sources of purpose rather than trying to hold on to the old one. Creating new routines intentionally, rather than assuming they will simply emerge on their own, can make the transition into retirement both healthier and more satisfying.

Travel matters too, and so does simply spending time with the people you love, and I do not want anything in this chapter to suggest otherwise. Rest, travel, and time with family are important parts of a well-lived retirement, and this book has spent a great deal of effort helping you build the financial freedom to enjoy exactly that. Retirement also creates a real opportunity to strengthen relationships that may have received less attention during busy working years. Investing time in family, friendships, grandchildren, neighbors, and the broader community often becomes one of the most rewarding uses of this new freedom. Conversations become less hurried. Time with grandchildren becomes more available. Friendships that had been postponed can be renewed. These ordinary moments frequently become some of the most meaningful rewards of financial independence. But rest and travel work best as part of a fuller life, not as the entire substance of it. A retirement built entirely around leisure, with nothing underneath it to engage the mind, tends to run out of momentum faster than people expect.

Retirement can also become one of life's greatest opportunities for learning, and none of it has to be formal. Reading, attending lectures, studying history, learning a language, mastering new technology, or developing a creative skill can all keep curiosity and confidence growing well into later life. Curiosity, in my experience, is what keeps people engaged with life itself.

There is real research behind this concern, and I think it is worth sharing rather than simply asserting, with the right amount of caution about what it actually shows. Studies following older adults over many years have found that people who remain socially connected, mentally engaged, physically active, and maintain a sense of purpose tend to experience healthier aging and a lower risk of cognitive decline. None of this guarantees a particular outcome for any individual person. But together, these habits are consistently linked with better overall well-being, which is reason enough to take them seriously. This research matters most, I think, in the context of losing a spouse. Long-term studies have found that widows and widowers face a meaningfully elevated risk of cognitive decline compared with those who remain married, a difference associated not only with grief itself but also with the reduced social engagement that often follows the loss of a spouse. One study found that even when widowed individuals maintained the same amount of social contact as before, they still experienced greater loneliness, because a spouse's companionship is not fully replaceable by other relationships, however close. I do not raise this to frighten anyone. I raise it because it is worth planning for, the same way this entire book has encouraged you to plan for every other significant stage of life.

That is the real argument for treating retirement as a shift rather than an ending. Financial independence, the subject of an earlier chapter, lets you decide how to spend your time without the constraint of needing a paycheck. That freedom is valuable, but freedom by itself is not the same as purpose. Purpose is what you choose to do with that freedom once you have it. The people I have known who thrived in retirement were not necessarily the ones with the most money. They were the ones who walked into retirement with something to move toward, not just something they were leaving behind.

Retirement plans should also remain flexible. Interests change, health changes, and opportunities appear that could not have been anticipated while working. There is no reason to build a rigid schedule for the next twenty or thirty years. What matters is staying open to new ways of finding meaning as life continues to evolve.

If you are approaching this stage of life, I would encourage you to think about it well before the actual day arrives, the same way you would think through any other major financial decision in this book. What will genuinely engage you once the structure of a career is gone? Who will you stay connected to, and how will you make sure that connection continues intentionally rather than by accident? These questions do not have a single right answer, and the answer will look different for every reader. But asking them in advance, rather than discovering the gap after retirement has already begun, is one of the most important things you can do.

Retirement also creates the opportunity to appreciate what earlier years of discipline made possible. The pressure to build a career gradually gives way to the freedom to enjoy family, friendships, health, learning, travel, and ordinary moments that once seemed too easy to postpone. Gratitude often becomes one of the richest rewards of financial independence.

I no longer think of retirement as leaving something behind. I think of it as gaining the freedom to invest my time where it matters most. For me, that has included writing, learning, spending time with family, managing our investments, and continuing to grow in ways that a full-time career no longer allowed.

A successful retirement is measured not simply by how long your money lasts, but by how fully you continue to live. Financial independence gives you the freedom to choose. Purpose gives that freedom meaning.

Financial independence creates the opportunity to live with greater freedom. The next step is learning how to turn that freedom into a reliable stream of income that can support the life you have worked so hard to build.

CHAPTER FIFTEEN

Turning a Lifetime of Savings into a Lifetime of Income

Saving for retirement and generating reliable income in retirement are two entirely different disciplines. Most of this book, up to this point, has focused on the first one, accumulating wealth. Building a retirement income plan is the delicate work of converting decades of accumulated savings into a sustainable paycheck that must last for the rest of your life, without knowing in advance exactly how long that life will be. It is one of the most complex financial exercises most people ever undertake, and it deserves the same deliberate planning as every other strategy covered here.

A sound retirement income plan is rarely built from a single source. It is layered, drawing from multiple income streams at once, each with its own timing, tax treatment, and purpose. Social Security, discussed earlier, forms a foundational layer, and its timing shapes the trajectory of everything else. Systematic withdrawals from taxable, traditional tax-deferred, and Roth accounts provide another layer. For some retirees, a pension offers a third. And for us, annuities became a deliberate additional layer, chosen for a specific purpose I will explain shortly.

One of the more overlooked opportunities in retirement income planning is the window that may open between leaving full-time work and beginning Social Security benefits and required minimum distributions. Social Security does not begin automatically when you stop working. Individuals generally choose when to claim within the available age range. Required minimum distributions from traditional IRAs and most employer-sponsored retirement accounts generally begin at an age established by federal law, currently age seventy-three for many retirees and age seventy-five for people born in 1960 or later. Roth IRAs do not require distributions during the original owner's lifetime. The exact timing should always be confirmed under the rules in effect when retirement approaches.

Rather than treating this quiet stretch as merely a bridge to cross, you can use it strategically. For our household, this window became the time to execute partial Roth IRA conversions each year, converting a portion of traditional, pre-tax retirement savings into Roth accounts while our overall income was lower than it would be later. Roth conversions also require attention to the applicable five-year rules, particularly for individuals who may need access to converted amounts before age fifty-nine and a half. The tax treatment of a conversion and the requirements for a qualified Roth distribution are related but separate considerations. Money converted during those lower-income years is taxed in the year of conversion. If the conversion is completed while the household is in a lower tax bracket than it would otherwise face later, it may reduce future taxable required distributions and improve lifetime tax flexibility. But the result is not guaranteed. A conversion can also increase the portion of Social Security benefits subject to taxation, raise Medicare income-related premiums in a later year, and create state income-tax consequences. The decision should therefore be evaluated using the household's complete tax picture rather than the federal tax bracket alone.

I want to be careful here, because Roth conversions are not a universal cure, and the strategy requires precise calculations tailored to your personal numbers. The right amount to convert in any given year depends on your current and expected future tax brackets, the size of your traditional retirement accounts, the age at which required minimum distributions will begin, your Social Security claiming strategy, Medicare premium thresholds, charitable intentions, filing status, state tax rules, and the amount of cash available outside the retirement account to pay the resulting tax. It should also consider what may happen after the death of one spouse, when the survivor may eventually file as a single taxpayer while receiving much of the same retirement income. This is an area where working with a qualified tax professional or financial advisor to run the actual numbers for your specific situation is worth every dollar it costs. There is often a valuable planning window early in retirement when partial Roth conversions may reduce lifetime taxes or provide greater flexibility later. That opportunity may become less attractive after Social Security and required minimum distributions increase taxable income, but it does not necessarily disappear entirely. The benefit must be recalculated each year, because tax laws, income, account values, and personal circumstances can change.

Annuities became part of our income plan for a different reason entirely, and I want to explain that choice candidly, because annuities are a mixed topic among financial professionals, and for good reason. An annuity is a contract with an insurance company under which a lump sum or series of payments may be exchanged for income beginning immediately or at a future date. Depending on the contract selected, payments may continue for a fixed period, for one lifetime, or for the joint lives of two people. Any guarantee depends on the terms of the contract and the claims-paying ability of the issuing insurance company.

For our family, adding an annuity served three distinct purposes. The first was psychological. Having a portion of our baseline living expenses covered by a guaranteed check, regardless of market volatility or headlines, provided a level of peace that a volatile stock portfolio alone could not replicate. The second was timing. We structured our annuity purchases during a period of elevated interest rates, securing higher payout rates than were generally available in earlier, lower-rate environments. The third was income diversification itself, distinct from investment diversification. By combining Social Security, portfolio distributions, and contractual annuity payments, no single income source carried the full weight of our lifestyle.

The payment amount is only one part of the decision. A fixed payment may provide stability but gradually lose purchasing power as prices rise. Married couples should also consider whether income continues for the surviving spouse and how choosing joint-life protection affects the initial payment. Some contracts provide inflation adjustments, guaranteed payment periods, or death benefits, but each additional feature may reduce the income received or increase the cost. The appropriate design depends on whether the primary goal is maximum current income, protection for a spouse, liquidity, inflation protection, or leaving assets to heirs.

The trade-offs deserve equally direct treatment. Annuities vary considerably in liquidity. Money used to purchase an immediate income annuity is generally committed in exchange for the promised payment stream and may no longer be freely accessible. Other annuity contracts may allow withdrawals, but surrender charges, taxes, contractual limits, or penalties can apply, and readers should understand exactly what access to principal remains before committing funds. Fees and structures vary considerably across insurance products as well, and for most retirees, a straightforward annuity designed to cover essential baseline costs is more appropriate than a complex product loaded with multiple riders. Because an annuity's guarantees depend primarily on the claims-paying ability of the issuing insurance company rather than federal deposit insurance, the financial strength of the insurer also matters. A retiree considering a substantial annuity purchase should review the insurer's ratings, understand applicable state guaranty-association limits, and consider whether placing too much retirement income with one company creates unnecessary concentration risk.

In practice, this means looking for top-tier ratings from the major independent agencies, such as A.M. Best, S&P, or Moody's, before committing to a contract. Depending on the size of the annuity, it may also be worth verifying strength across more than one insurance company rather than placing the full amount with a single carrier. For me, timing mattered as much as the rating. I purchased when interest rates were elevated, which meant a stronger payout rate locked in from the start. That kind of payout becomes especially advantageous if you live well into your eighties or nineties, since the payments simply continue for as long as you do.

One mistake I want to address directly, because I have seen it repeatedly, is spending far too conservatively out of fear, to the point where decades of disciplined saving are never actually enjoyed. Some retirees, having spent a lifetime building financial discipline, find it difficult to shift into spending mode, even when their plan clearly supports it. The habits that build wealth are not the same habits that allow you to enjoy it. If you have structured your income plan thoughtfully, stress-tested it against conservative assumptions, and built in appropriate safety margins, then the money is there to be used. Wealth preserved purely out of fear is wealth wasted.

The opposite mistake is equally dangerous: drawing down capital too aggressively in the early, active years of retirement, without accounting for how the order of investment returns can affect a portfolio. Withdrawing heavily from a declining portfolio may require selling more shares at depressed prices and leave fewer assets available to participate in a later recovery. This interaction between withdrawals and the order in which investment returns occur is known as sequence-of-returns risk. Two retirees can earn similar average returns over time and still experience very different outcomes if one encounters significant losses near the beginning of retirement. No withdrawal percentage should be treated as an automatic guarantee. A sustainable amount depends on retirement length, portfolio composition, market conditions, inflation, taxes, spending flexibility, and the dependable income available from other sources.

Some retirees choose to align dependable income sources, such as Social Security, pensions, and appropriate annuity payments, with essential expenses. This can reduce the amount that must be withdrawn from market-based investments during a downturn.

However, the plan should also account for inflation, because not every income source increases with the cost of living, and for the possibility that expenses may rise later because of healthcare, housing, or long-term-care needs.

The order in which retirement accounts are used can also matter. Withdrawals from traditional retirement accounts are generally taxable, qualified Roth withdrawals may be tax-free, and taxable investment accounts have their own rules for dividends and capital gains. There is no single withdrawal order that works for every household. In some years, drawing from more than one type of account may help manage tax brackets, preserve flexibility, reduce future required distributions, or avoid unnecessarily increasing Medicare premiums. The objective should not be simply to minimize this year's tax bill, but to manage taxes over the full retirement period. The plan should also be tested for the period after the first spouse dies. Household expenses may not decline proportionately, while one Social Security benefit may end, filing status may change, tax brackets may narrow, and the survivor may need to manage the income plan alone.

A retirement income plan should also include room for adjustment. Spending may be higher during the active early years of retirement, lower during quieter years, and higher again if healthcare or support needs increase. Market conditions may also require temporary restraint. Establishing which expenses are essential and which are discretionary makes it easier to reduce portfolio withdrawals during difficult periods without disrupting the basic standard of living. Flexibility can be as important to the durability of a retirement plan as the initial withdrawal amount.

There is one more habit of mind worth carrying into this stage of planning, something I have come to appreciate more with each passing year. Investors often ask which fund, or which mix of funds, delivers the best long-term growth. The honest answer is that the number changes depending on how far back you look, and understanding why matters more than memorizing any single figure.

Consider a diversified portfolio built from broad-market, growth-oriented, international, and cash holdings. Its reported annualized return can look very different depending on whether the measurement begins before a major decline, near the bottom of one, or during a prolonged period of rising markets. A recent ten-year result may be considerably stronger than a longer result that includes additional recessions and market declines. Nothing about the current portfolio needs to change for the historical picture to look different. Only the starting and ending dates have changed. That is why past performance should always be examined across multiple periods and market conditions rather than treated as a dependable forecast of what retirement assets will earn in the future.

The lesson I want you to take from this is not about investing alone. It applies directly to the income plan we have been discussing throughout this chapter. When you evaluate a fund, an advisor's pitch, or your own retirement projections, ask what period the underlying number covers, and ask what it would look like if you moved the window. If the answer changes drastically, treat the figure with appropriate caution. I did not build my own retirement income approach around chasing the highest historical average I could find. I built it around a plan designed to withstand both kinds of years, the good ones and the difficult ones, because once an income strategy is already in motion, durability and reliability matter more than chasing an extra point or two of return in a strong year.

Building a retirement income plan is not a single decision made in the year you retire. It is an ongoing process, revisited as spending changes, tax laws evolve, markets move, health needs develop, and one spouse's circumstances affect the other. What matters most is not any single tactic in this chapter, but approaching retirement income with the same intentionality you used to accumulate the money in the first place.

The goal is not simply to preserve every dollar indefinitely, nor is it to spend without regard for the future. It is to create a durable and flexible income plan that allows you to meet your obligations, adapt to uncertainty, support the surviving spouse, and enjoy the life you spent decades working to build.

CHAPTER SIXTEEN

Keeping More of What You Earn

The previous chapter focused on turning savings into income. This chapter focuses on a quieter but equally important question: how much of that income actually stays yours. Tax planning means arranging financial decisions within the law so that you do not pay more than necessary. It is not evasion, and it does not mean eliminating every dollar of tax you owe. The aim is to manage taxes over an entire financial lifetime while preserving flexibility for the years ahead, not to win any single year. Every chapter in this book, from the habits described early on to the retirement income plan in the previous chapter, feeds directly into this one. Tax planning is woven through nearly every decision already discussed rather than standing apart from them.

After leaving corporate life, I began looking at these decisions as parts of one financial picture rather than as separate transactions. Using the retirement projection tools available through my brokerage, I estimated the income we would need, how claiming Social Security at seventy would affect the years still available for

Roth conversions, and what our taxable income might look like once required minimum distributions begin at seventy-five under current law. Those projections helped me coordinate five fixed annuities, spread among three highly rated insurance companies, with IRA withdrawals and funds available in taxable investment accounts, while remaining mindful of the possible effect on future Medicare premiums.

Withdrawal rules are among the more unforgiving areas of tax planning because mistakes can create specific and avoidable costs. A taxable distribution from a traditional IRA or workplace retirement plan before age fifty-nine and a half is generally subject to ordinary income tax and an additional ten percent federal tax unless an exception applies. The additional tax applies only to the taxable portion of the distribution, and the available exceptions differ between IRAs and employer-sponsored plans.

Leaving a career at age fifty-five does not automatically provide penalty-free access to an IRA. Under the provision commonly called the Rule of 55, distributions may avoid the additional ten percent tax when an employee separates from service during or after the calendar year in which the employee turns fifty-five. The exception generally applies only to the retirement plan maintained by the employer from which the employee separated, not to an IRA or automatically to plans left with previous employers. Certain qualified public-safety employees may qualify at an earlier age, and plan rules must also permit the withdrawal.

Another exception permits a properly calculated series of substantially equal periodic payments. Once begun, the schedule generally must continue until the later of five years or age fifty-nine and a half. Changing the arrangement prematurely can cause the additional tax to be imposed retroactively, with interest. Anyone considering this strategy should have the calculation and requirements reviewed before the first distribution is taken, not after.

Once you are past fifty-nine and a half, and particularly once you approach the required minimum distribution age discussed in the previous chapter, the challenge shifts from avoiding penalties to managing timing. The first required distribution may generally be postponed until April 1 of the following year, but doing so can place two required distributions into that following calendar year. That concentration of taxable income may increase the household's tax bracket, the taxation of Social Security benefits, or future Medicare premiums, so weigh the consequences of postponement rather than treating it as an automatic advantage.

Which accounts you draw from, and in what order, in any given year, can meaningfully change your total tax burden over the course of retirement. This is where the layered income plan described in the previous chapter becomes a tax strategy as much as an income strategy. Traditional account withdrawals are taxable as ordinary income. Roth IRA earnings are generally tax-free when the applicable five-year requirement has been met and the distribution occurs after age fifty-nine and a half, because of disability or death, or for another qualifying purpose. Contributions and converted amounts follow separate ordering and penalty rules. Taxable brokerage accounts carry their own rules around dividends and capital gains. In any given year, the mix of accounts you draw from can be adjusted to manage your total taxable income, which in turn affects far more than just your federal tax bracket.

This is where Medicare's income-related monthly adjustment amount, generally known as IRMAA, deserves real attention.

IRMAA is technically not an income tax but an additional amount added to Medicare Part B and Part D costs when modified adjusted gross income exceeds annually adjusted thresholds. Social Security generally relies on tax-return information from two years earlier, which is why a large IRA withdrawal, Roth conversion, capital gain, or other income event can increase Medicare costs two years later, often catching people by surprise because the connection between the two events is not obvious in the moment. Medicare premiums and IRMAA brackets can change annually, so current thresholds should always be checked before a major transaction.

The effect is not necessarily permanent. IRMAA is recalculated each year as newer tax-return information becomes available. Someone whose income has fallen because of a qualifying life-changing event, such as stopping or reducing work, marriage, divorce, or the death of a spouse, may ask Social Security to reconsider the adjustment using more recent income information through Form SSA-44. It is worth knowing that appeal exists, because many retirees pay a higher premium longer than necessary simply because they were unaware the option existed.

The previous chapter introduced Roth conversions as a strategy for the gap years before Social Security and required distributions begin. That window is not the end of the story. Roth conversions remain relevant well beyond those years. Even after required minimum distributions begin, further conversions of remaining traditional balances can still make sense in some years, depending on your overall tax picture, though the required distribution itself cannot be converted and must be satisfied first. A Roth conversion completed under current law generally cannot be reversed later simply because the tax cost was higher than expected or the converted investments declined in value, which makes advance calculation especially important. The tax created by a conversion should also be considered alongside cash available outside the retirement account, because using retirement assets to pay the tax reduces the amount that actually reaches the Roth account. Thinking of Roth conversions as a strategy limited to a single window early in retirement misses the larger point. It is a tool available across many years of retirement, one to be revisited annually as your income, tax law, and account balances change, rather than a decision made once and set aside.

Charitable giving offers another meaningful opportunity. Beginning at age seventy and a half, an eligible taxpayer may direct a qualified charitable distribution from an IRA to an eligible charitable organization. A qualifying transfer can count toward all or part of an IRA required minimum distribution while remaining excluded from adjusted gross income, subject to an annually adjusted limit. It is worth noting that this age, seventy and a half, is earlier than the required minimum distribution age itself, currently seventy-three or seventy-five depending on birth year. For anyone charitably inclined, that gap creates a real head start, an opportunity to reduce a traditional IRA balance tax-free for a few years before required distributions even begin. The transfer must generally move directly from the IRA custodian to the charity, and not every charitable organization is eligible, so the account and recipient should be confirmed before funds are transferred. This can be more tax-efficient than taking a taxable distribution and then donating the proceeds, particularly for someone who does not itemize deductions, though the same amount cannot be excluded from income as a qualified charitable distribution and also claimed separately as a charitable deduction.

A separate technique applies to taxable, non-retirement accounts. Donating appreciated investments held there directly to an eligible charity, rather than selling them and donating the cash, may avoid recognizing the embedded capital gain. When applicable requirements are met, particularly the holding-period rules, an itemizing taxpayer may also qualify for a charitable deduction based on fair market value. Deduction limits, substantiation requirements, the type of property donated, and the receiving organization all matter, so the transaction should be confirmed before the asset is transferred.

Tax planning is not limited to retirement accounts. In taxable investment accounts, realizing losses may offset realized capital gains and, within federal limits, a portion of ordinary income. In a low-income year, intentionally realizing some long-term capital gains may also be advantageous if they fall within a favorable capital-gains bracket. Neither strategy should be driven by taxes alone. Investment suitability, portfolio allocation, holding periods, and rules that can disallow or defer a loss must all be considered before a trade is made.

Where an investment is held can matter almost as much as which investment is selected. Interest-producing assets, tax-efficient stock funds, municipal securities, and investments expected to appreciate may receive different tax treatment depending on whether they are held in a traditional retirement account, a Roth account, or a taxable brokerage account. Thoughtful asset location can improve after-tax results without requiring a more aggressive investment strategy.

Tax planning should also consider what happens after the death of one spouse. A surviving spouse may eventually move from married filing jointly to single filing status while continuing to receive a substantial portion of the household's prior income. That can expose the survivor to narrower tax brackets, different Medicare income thresholds, and a higher effective tax burden. Roth conversions, beneficiary planning, and the structure of retirement income should therefore be evaluated for both spouses, not only for the years when they are filing jointly.

Tax planning should also include the people who may inherit retirement accounts. Depending on the beneficiary and the applicable rules, many nonspouse beneficiaries may be required to empty an inherited retirement account within a limited period, potentially creating significant taxable income during their own highest-earning years. Beneficiary designations, Roth conversions, charitable intentions, and the types of assets left to each heir should therefore be considered together rather than as separate decisions.

Even a sound strategy can create problems if the resulting tax is not paid on time. Retirement-account distributions, Roth conversions, investment gains, pensions, and other income may require additional withholding or estimated tax payments during the year. Tax planning should therefore address not only how much tax may ultimately be owed, but also when and how it will be paid, so that avoidable underpayment penalties do not undermine the strategy.

None of these strategies exist in isolation, and none of them should be evaluated using a single number in a single year. A withdrawal decision that looks efficient in isolation might trigger higher Social Security taxation, a higher IRMAA tier, or a larger state tax bill, depending on your full financial picture. This is precisely why tax planning belongs alongside a broader retirement income plan rather than being treated as a separate, occasional task. The specific thresholds, brackets, and limits referenced throughout this chapter change from year to year, sometimes significantly, so the principles described here are meant to outlast any particular year's numbers.

The real measure of tax planning is how effectively your decisions preserve after-tax wealth, financial flexibility, and dependable income throughout your lifetime, and for the people who may eventually inherit what remains. How little you paid in any one isolated year proves almost nothing. Keeping more of what you earn requires the same discipline as earning, saving, and investing it, but it also requires the humility to recognize when the rules are complex enough to justify professional guidance.

These four chapters, taken together, cover the financial mechanics of living on what you have built: when to claim Social Security, what retirement itself is for, how to turn savings into income, and how to keep as much of that income as the law allows. What remains is not a mechanical question at all. The final chapters of this book turn to something less easily measured: teaching what you know to the people who come after you, and deciding what you actually want to leave behind.

PART FIVE

BEYOND WEALTH

CHAPTER SEVENTEEN

Teaching the Next Generation About Money

Everything discussed so far in this book has focused on building your own financial foundation. This chapter addresses something distinct, and considerably more challenging: helping someone else build theirs, while resisting the natural urge to build it for them.

Children often learn more from what they observe than from what they are told. They watch how their parents spend, save, borrow, give, and react to financial setbacks. Long before they understand budgets or investing, they are already forming beliefs about money simply by watching the adults around them. The example we set is often our first, and most influential, financial lesson.

The debt lessons described earlier in this book, involving our sons' early experiences with student loans and vehicle purchases, did not begin in college or at a car dealership. They began years earlier, when both of our sons were in high school and took on their first part-time jobs. From that point forward, we gave them full autonomy to manage their earned income. They could spend it or save it as they chose, and like most teenagers encountering independent money for the first time, they made mistakes. I offered guidance along the way, sharing how I would evaluate a choice, but watching your child make a flawed financial decision when you have the capacity to step in and fix it is genuinely difficult. The parental instinct to bail them out is strong. Resisting it is one of the more uncomfortable, yet vital, duties of parenting.

Earning that first paycheck, I have come to believe, mattered just as much as learning how to manage it. Money earned through personal effort carries a different meaning than money simply received. It teaches that income is connected to time, responsibility, and work, making later lessons about budgeting and saving much easier to understand.

We also tried to make money a normal topic of conversation rather than something mysterious or avoided. We talked about budgeting, saving, investing, debt, and the reasons behind our financial decisions. Children do not need to know every detail of a family's finances, but understanding how thoughtful financial decisions are made prepares them to make their own. Those conversations did not happen only when a problem appeared. They became part of ordinary family life. Talking openly about saving for a goal, comparing financial choices, or explaining why one purchase made sense while another did not helped remove the mystery surrounding money and made financial decision-making feel like a normal life skill rather than a subject to avoid.

I remember clearly when our older son decided to get his first credit card. Like many young adults encountering open lines of credit, he did not fully grasp the underlying mechanics. He charged expenses against it without realizing that a purchase made today must be settled in full, or interest begins compounding against you.

It was a sharp, unpleasant awakening. My wife and I discussed how to respond, and we agreed not to intervene. We required him to work through the balance and the accumulated interest entirely on his own. It was difficult to watch, but it proved to be one of the most valuable lessons he ever learned, precisely because the discomfort was real, and the responsibility was solely his to carry.

Those lessons were never only about money. They were also lessons in responsibility, accountability, delayed gratification, and accepting the consequences of one's own decisions. Those qualities serve people well far beyond their financial lives.

What stood out to me was what happened with our younger son. Having closely observed his brother navigate that stress, he never made the same mistake himself. He absorbed the lesson secondhand simply by watching the consequences unfold, a compelling argument for allowing an older child to experience the natural results of a financial misstep. A lesson learned firsthand by one child often eliminates the need for the next child to relearn it.

This became our core philosophy throughout their formative years, across vehicles, credit, and daily budgeting: provide transparent guidance, explain our own reasoning, and let the final decision, along with its consequences, belong to them. This approach has to start young for a practical reason. A financial mistake made at seventeen, with a part-time job's paycheck on the line, is easily correctable. The exact same mistake made at thirty-five, with a mortgage, a family, or a business on the line, can be considerably more serious. Allowing children to make small, low-stakes mistakes early is one of the best ways to prepare them for the much larger decisions that come later. Those early mistakes also build confidence. A young person who learns how to recover from a financial error while the consequences are still manageable becomes less likely to panic when larger financial decisions arise later in life. Learning how to correct a mistake is every bit as valuable as learning how to avoid one.

That early, hands-off approach is a primary reason both of our sons matured into financially astute young adults. They understand financial mechanics not because I lectured them repeatedly, but because they experienced enough of the consequences themselves to internalize the lessons. As they stepped into adulthood, I continued to advise them, emphasizing the importance of building a liquid emergency fund, maximizing an employer's retirement match before allocating a dollar elsewhere, and applying the core habits outlined throughout this book. They have taken those principles and adapted them to their own lives, which is really the goal of all of this: not that they follow my exact instructions, but that they possess the analytical framework to make sound decisions on their own, in circumstances I will never fully see.

Financial wisdom also includes learning that money is for more than spending or saving. It can also be used to help others. Teaching children to give, whether through charitable causes, helping family members in need, or supporting their communities, reminds them that money is ultimately a tool to improve lives, not simply to accumulate possessions. Giving also teaches perspective. It reminds children that financial success carries responsibility as well as opportunity, and that wealth is measured not only by what we keep but also by how thoughtfully we use it to improve the lives of others.

I want to acknowledge something honestly, because I do not think it would be fair to close this chapter without saying it. The financial world our sons are building their adult lives in is genuinely more difficult than the one my wife and I started in. Housing costs, higher education expenses, and healthcare have generally risen faster than overall inflation over long periods, making disciplined saving considerably more challenging than it was for many previous generations. Technology has changed the landscape as well. Credit is easier to obtain, online shopping makes spending nearly effortless, social media constantly encourages comparison, and financial misinformation spreads quickly. Teaching young people how to evaluate financial information critically has become almost as important as teaching them how to budget or invest. I do not say any of this to discourage anyone reading this book on behalf of their own children. I say it because teaching the next generation about money today requires acknowledging that reality honestly, rather than pretending the path is as straightforward as it once was.

For readers raising children or helping guide grandchildren, a few strategies deserve particular attention early. Once a teenager has taxable compensation from wages or legitimate self-employment, a custodial Roth IRA can be opened for them. A parent or grandparent can contribute on the child's behalf, up to the amount of the child's own earned income for that year and subject to the annual Roth contribution limit. It does not matter who provides the money. What matters is that the child actually earned that much. Funding even a modest Roth IRA for a working teenager gives that money decades of tax-free compound growth, the kind of head start described earlier, one that is nearly impossible to replicate later in life. More important than the dollar amount contributed in any given year is establishing the habit of investing long before it feels necessary.

A 529 plan, discussed in earlier chapters, becomes considerably more valuable the earlier it is started, given how much compounding benefits from time. Under current law, families who worry about overfunding a 529, in case a child receives a scholarship or chooses a different path, have an additional option worth knowing about: unused 529 funds, up to a lifetime limit of thirty-five thousand dollars, can potentially be rolled over tax-free into a Roth IRA for the beneficiary, subject to several specific requirements, including that the 529 account must have been open for at least fifteen years and that the beneficiary must have sufficient earned income. The rules governing this rollover are detailed and worth confirming with a tax professional before relying on them, but the option itself has removed a longstanding concern for many families considering how much to save. And thinking seriously, well in advance, about where a child might eventually want to go to school, and what that will likely cost by the time they arrive there, is not premature planning. It is simply planning for a cost that could be substantial if college is the path they choose.

One of the quiet goals of good parenting is gradually making yourself less necessary in your children's financial decisions. Advice should become less about directing every choice and more about serving as a trusted sounding board when they ask for guidance. Independence, not dependence, is the measure of success.

Eventually, every parent reaches the point where financial decisions no longer belong to them. That is the true test of whether the lessons have taken root. Success is not measured by whether children make every decision exactly as we would. It is measured by whether they possess the judgment, discipline, and confidence to make thoughtful decisions on their own, long after our advice is no longer needed.

Looking back, I do not measure our success by whether our sons followed every piece of advice we offered. I measure it by the fact that they now think through financial decisions carefully, ask thoughtful questions, and accept responsibility for the choices they make. That was always the objective.

Neither of my sons has followed the path exactly as I would have laid it out. Both started contributing to a 401(k) later than I did. But the habits underneath the specific choices took hold. They understand enough to make saving a consistent part of their lives, and both are building real wealth on their own terms. My encouragement to any parent reading this is simple: keep teaching, even when the lessons do not land exactly as intended. They tend to land eventually, and what matters most is that your children grow into responsible adults.

Teaching the next generation about money depends less on the lessons you deliver than on the space you are willing to give them to learn those lessons themselves, at an age when the cost of learning is still small. That space, uncomfortable as it can be to provide, may be one of the more valuable things you ever give them.

CHAPTER EIGHTEEN

The Legacy You Leave

The previous chapter was about raising children who understand money while you are still there to guide them. This chapter is about what continues after you are no longer here. There is a meaningful difference between a legacy and an inheritance, and this entire book has been quietly building toward that distinction. An inheritance is what changes hands. A legacy is what shapes the person receiving it, long before anything actually changes hands, and long after it does.

The most meaningful legacy is rarely created through a document signed at the end of life. It is created while you are still here, through the time you invest in people, the conversations you have, and the example you consistently set. By the time an inheritance is received, much of the true legacy has already been passed on.

One lesson has become increasingly clear to me over the years: people rarely remember us because of what we owned. They remember whether we were present, whether we listened, whether we encouraged them, and whether we lived in a way that made them want to follow our example. Those everyday moments often become the most enduring part of a legacy.

This was embedded in me as a child, watching how my own parents carried themselves, the principles they lived by, the integrity they showed without ever announcing it. I have since watched that same thing happen beyond my own household, in my siblings' children and even their grandchildren, the same principles and the same way of living continuing forward, not because anyone sat them down and demanded it, but because they saw it lived out. I have found, in my own experience, that lecturing, applying pressure, or forcing a lesson rarely produces that kind of lasting result. Leading by example does. It is a slower way to teach, and a quieter one, but it tends to be the one that actually holds.

Money can be part of a legacy. It often is. But money alone has never been the thing I most wanted to pass down. What I have wanted to pass down, more than any account balance, is an understanding of where we come from, how we got to where we are, and enough of a sense of direction that the next generation can continue improving on the path rather than simply inheriting the endpoint. Legacy, understood this way, is not a single transfer at the end of a life but something built continuously, in the ordinary decisions and conversations that accumulate over an entire lifetime.

Values are at the center of that. The habits described throughout this book, living below your means, avoiding unnecessary debt, saving consistently, giving generously, are not really financial habits in isolation. They are expressions of values that existed long before any of us had money to manage, values centered on discipline, patience, honesty, and taking responsibility for your own decisions. Financial wisdom is only one part of the legacy we leave. Integrity, kindness, generosity, humility, resilience, and faith often shape future generations even more deeply than financial success does. Money may provide opportunities, but character determines how those opportunities are used. When I think about what I most want my sons, and my grandson after them, to carry forward, it is not a specific dollar figure. It is the reasoning behind the decisions, the why underneath the what, applied consistently enough that they can recognize it and use it themselves, in circumstances I cannot predict and will not be there to advise on directly.

That is part of why the earlier chapters in this book spent so much time on how, not just what. Anyone can be told to save money. Fewer people understand why living below your means creates freedom, why debt taken on without purpose becomes a quiet drag on everything else, or why time matters more than almost any other financial variable. A legacy built only on rules, followed without understanding, tends not to survive the first generation that encounters circumstances those rules did not anticipate. Every generation faces different challenges. Economic conditions change, technology changes, careers change, and opportunities change. A lasting legacy should provide principles that remain relevant even when circumstances do not. Teaching someone how to think prepares them for a future that no one can fully predict.

I have never viewed wealth as something we truly own forever. We are stewards of it for a period of time. Stewardship also means recognizing that wealth has a purpose beyond preservation. It should support the people we love, reflect the values we hold, and, where possible, leave the next generation better prepared rather than simply better funded. Our responsibility is to manage it wisely, use it thoughtfully, enjoy it responsibly, and leave it in better condition than we found it whenever possible. That perspective changes the conversation from ownership to responsibility.

Financial legacy has a structural side as well, and I want to address it honestly, because I do not think a chapter on legacy is complete without it. My wife and I established an irrevocable trust structure to benefit our two sons and our grandson, accompanied by updated healthcare proxies and durable powers of attorney. We appointed our sons as trustees, so they would be actively involved in managing the multi-generational protection of what we built, rather than simply receiving something they had no hand in shaping.

Under current law, many non-spouse beneficiaries are generally required to distribute inherited retirement accounts within ten years, subject to several exceptions. Between rules like that one and shifting tax exemptions, how assets pass down matters just as much as what passes down. Estate planning is an evolving framework, not a static document drafted once and left in a drawer, and it requires periodic review with a qualified estate attorney and tax professional to navigate state laws, protect assets from external liabilities, and prevent unnecessary tax erosion for the people who eventually inherit them. Good estate planning does more than distribute assets efficiently. It reduces uncertainty, protects loved ones, minimizes unnecessary conflict, and makes an already difficult time a little easier for the family left behind.

Estate planning prepares more than legal documents. It prepares your family. Clear conversations about your intentions, your values, and the reasons behind important decisions can prevent misunderstandings and unnecessary conflict after you are gone. Sometimes the greatest gift is not the plan itself, but making sure those you love understand why you created it. Preparing heirs is often more important than preparing the inheritance itself. Financial knowledge, sound judgment, and shared family values help ensure that what is passed down becomes a lasting benefit rather than a temporary advantage.

I recognize that not everyone reading this book will have the same tools available, the same family structure, or the same priorities. What one family needs from an estate plan, whether a trust, a will, clear beneficiary designations, or guardianship provisions, is different from what another family needs, and the right approach depends entirely on your own circumstances. What matters is not replicating anyone else's specific structure. What matters is giving this the same deliberate attention you have given everything else described in this book, well before it becomes urgent, rather than leaving it as an afterthought.

Every family has stories worth preserving. The sacrifices that were made, the obstacles that were overcome, the traditions that shaped a family, and the lessons learned through both success and failure can easily disappear within a generation unless someone intentionally shares them. Recording those stories, whether through conversations, letters, photographs, or books, becomes part of the legacy itself. Those stories do more than preserve history. They give future generations a sense of identity and belonging. Knowing where a family came from, what it endured, and what it valued often provides strength during challenges that future generations will inevitably face.

I think often of the individuals whose legacy shaped my own compass long before I realized I was absorbing it. My parents did not leave behind any real financial assets. They came to this country at a late age and had to rebuild their entire lives from nothing. It was not easy for them, giving up everything they had built to that point. They did it so my siblings and I could have the opportunity to grow up in a country with far more open doors than the one they left behind. What they provided instead of money was a way of approaching life that was disciplined, resilient, and deeply grounded in faith, integrity, and family. That foundation is what I carried with me across an ocean as a young immigrant, and it became the engine that built an entire career, a home, and a legacy on top of it. Wealth can be depleted in a single generation of poor decisions, but the internal discipline required to create and sustain it endures. I would consider myself fortunate if the values passed down to me prove equally durable in my own sons and grandson.

In the end, people may remember what you left them, but they are far more likely to remember how you lived, how you treated others, what you stood for, and how your example influenced their own lives. Those memories often become the part of a legacy that lasts the longest.

I have come to believe that the greatest legacy is not measured by the size of an estate, but by the number of lives made stronger because we were here.

A legacy is not something you leave behind on a single day. It accumulates, quietly, in the conversations you have, the example you set, the structures you put in place, and the values you demonstrate more consistently than you announce them. The question worth asking is not whether you will leave a legacy. Everyone does, whether intentionally or by default. The real question is whether the legacy you are building right now, in the ordinary decisions of an ordinary week, is the one you actually want the people who come after you to inherit.

CHAPTER NINETEEN

Wealth in Service of a Life Well Lived

This book opened with a simple idea: money is a tool, not the destination. Eighteen chapters later, after habits and debt and investing and insurance and Social Security and taxes and legacy, I want to return to that same idea, because everything in between was really just an elaboration of it. None of that discipline was ever meant to be the point. It was meant to build something. This final chapter is about what that something actually is.

Now that I am on the far side of the career, planning, and saving described throughout this book, I have come to believe this: live your life. Live it fully, and live it now. Not recklessly, and not without the discipline this entire book has argued for. But do not mistake discipline for deprivation. I never stopped spending on the things that bring me happiness, and nothing will stop me now, because I understand something I did not fully understand when I was younger: we pass through this life once. None of that is a license for carelessness. It is a reason to actually use what you have built, rather than guarding it indefinitely against a future that is never guaranteed to arrive.

One of the greatest lessons I learned is that financial wisdom is not found at either extreme. It is not reckless spending, and it is not endless accumulation. It is finding the balance between preparing responsibly for tomorrow and fully appreciating the opportunities available today.

There is a difference worth naming here, because it is easy to confuse the two. Short-term happiness is the new car, the thing you believe will finally make you feel that you have arrived. It rarely does, not for long. The happiness that actually lasts tends to come from somewhere else entirely, from the things you can do and enjoy today that you may not be able to do or enjoy tomorrow. A trip taken while you and the people you love are still healthy enough to take it. An afternoon given fully to someone, without your mind pulled in six directions at once. A moment you are actually present for, rather than one you are simply passing through on the way to something else.

Health, time, and relationships are the three forms of wealth that become more valuable with every year that passes. Money can help protect them, but it cannot replace them once they are lost. That is why I count taking care of your health as part of financial planning, and one of the best investments you will ever make.

I think often about how quickly windows close, and how rarely we notice while they are still open. I had a friend, the same one I mentioned earlier in this book, who died of a heart attack at sixty-one. In the months before he died, he had called me a few times, and I kept meaning to call him back. I never did. Within a week of his last call, he was gone. I tell you this not for sympathy, but because it is the clearest lesson I know about believing you have more time than you actually do. We assume there will be another opportunity, another call, another visit, another year. Sometimes there is. Sometimes there is not, and the only honest response to that uncertainty is to live deliberately inside whatever window is currently open, rather than assuming it will stay open indefinitely.

I have tried to carry that lesson forward, and it has genuinely changed how I approach nearly everything, not just money. It has changed how I spend my mornings, how I show up for the people I love, and how seriously I take the ordinary, unremarkable days that, strung together, quietly become an entire life. None of this diminishes anything discussed earlier. If anything, it is the reason for all of it. You build financial security so that when the window is open, you are actually free to walk through it, rather than watching it close from behind a desk you cannot afford to leave.

I want to say something directly about attitude, because it matters as much as the strategies I have described. I have tried to live with a positive, grateful outlook through every stage of my life, including the more difficult ones, and I believe that outlook has shaped the outcome as much as any financial decision I ever made. Gratitude is not something that arrives automatically once you have enough money. I have met people with a great deal of money who felt no gratitude, and people with far less money who felt an abundance of it. Gratitude, like the financial habits described throughout this book, is a practice, chosen deliberately and repeated consistently, not a reward that shows up once the numbers are large enough.

Gratitude also changes how we measure success. Instead of constantly comparing ourselves with people who have more, we begin appreciating the opportunities already in front of us. That shift in perspective often creates a greater sense of abundance than another increase in income ever could.

One lesson became clearer to me as the years passed: the greatest satisfaction rarely came from accumulating more. It came from helping someone else. Whether through mentoring, sharing knowledge, volunteering, writing, or simply being available when someone needed encouragement, service gave purpose to everything financial success had made possible.

Faith has also been an anchor throughout my life. It has reminded me that while careful planning is important, not everything is within our control. We do our part with discipline, integrity, and gratitude, then accept with humility that some outcomes remain beyond our ability to predict or manage.

When I look back over my life, I do not remember the years by investment returns or account balances. I remember the people who shared those years with me: family dinners, conversations, friendships, simple acts of kindness, and time spent with those who mattered most. Those ordinary moments became the life I was building all along. They are the returns that never appear on a financial statement.

Retirement, or what I have called my second act, has not been a period of winding down for me. It has been a period of discovery. I found writing in it, something I did not fully know I needed until I stepped away from the career that had occupied me for nearly four decades. I continue to read, to learn, to stay engaged with the world in ways that keep me sharp and, I believe, keep me healthier than I might otherwise be. I would encourage every reader approaching this stage of life not to treat it as an ending, a time to stop reaching for anything new, but as an open invitation to discover what has been waiting, quietly, underneath the career the whole time.

Passion and motivation do not have an expiration date tied to a particular birthday. They can continue long after the working years end.

Financial independence does not eliminate every problem, but it can free you from the constant anxiety of wondering whether you have enough. Beyond that point, the challenge changes. It is no longer learning how to earn more. It is learning to recognize when you already have enough and allowing yourself to enjoy it. Knowing when you have enough may be one of the most difficult financial decisions any of us ever make. There will always be another investment to pursue, another milestone to reach, or another reason to postpone enjoyment. At some point, wisdom is recognizing that the purpose of financial independence is to support life, not delay living it.

Before I close, I want to leave you with one question, because I think it stays with a person longer than any advice I could give directly. If your life ended sooner than you expected, would the people you love remember someone who was always preparing to live, or someone who truly did?

Look back over everything this book has covered, and a shape emerges. We began with what money actually is. We moved into the habits that build it, the protections that guard it, the decisions that carry you through retirement, and finally, what outlasts all of it. None of those parts stand alone. They were always one idea, examined from five different angles.

Build wisely. Save consistently. Invest patiently. Protect your family. Give generously. Continue learning. Love the people around you well. Be grateful for ordinary days. Leave those who come after you better prepared than you were. If this book encourages you to do those things, then it has accomplished exactly what I hoped it would.

If there is one hope I have for every reader, it is that the financial principles in these pages provide more than security. I hope they give you the freedom to spend your time where it matters most, to strengthen your relationships, to continue learning, to serve others, and to live with purpose and gratitude. That, to me, is the true return on a lifetime of careful financial planning.

Money was never the destination.

A life well lived always was.

Appendix: Retirement Planning Worksheets

YOUR RETIREMENT INCOME PLAN

List the income you expect to receive. Separate dependable income from income that may fluctuate or require withdrawals from savings.

DEPENDABLE INCOME	Monthly	Annual
Social Security	$________	$________
Pension	$________	$________
Annuity income	$________	$________
Other dependable income	$________	$________
Total Dependable Income	**$__________**	**$__________**

ADDITIONAL INCOME	Monthly	Annual
Retirement-account withdrawals	$________	$________
Taxable investment withdrawals	$________	$________
Employment or consulting	$________	$________
Rental or other income	$________	$________
Total Additional Income	**$__________**	**$__________**

TOTAL EXPECTED INCOME	**$__________**	**$__________**

YOUR RETIREMENT SPENDING PLAN

Estimate what you expect to spend. Separating essential from discretionary expenses shows where adjustments can be made when circumstances change.

ESSENTIAL EXPENSES	**Monthly**	**Annual**
Housing and property taxes	$________	$________
Utilities	$________	$________
Food and household expenses	$________	$________
Healthcare and insurance	$________	$________
Transportation	$________	$________
Income taxes	$________	$________
Debt payments	$________	$________
Other essential expenses	$________	$________
Total Essential Expenses	**$__________**	**$__________**

DISCRETIONARY EXPENSES	**Monthly**	**Annual**
Travel and entertainment	$________	$________
Dining and recreation	$________	$________
Gifts and charitable giving	$________	$________
Other discretionary expenses	$________	$________
Total Discretionary Expenses	**$__________**	**$__________**

YOUR ANNUAL PICTURE

Total Expected Income	$____________________
Total Expected Expenses	$____________________
Annual Surplus or Shortfall	$____________________

Revisit this plan once a year, and after any major change.

Notes on Sources

The stories in this book are my own, told from memory. Where I have relied on published research, government rules, or data compiled by others, those sources are listed here by chapter.

Tax rules, contribution limits, benefit formulas, premium thresholds, and cost estimates change, often every year. Every figure cited in this book reflects the information available as the book went to press. Before acting on anything described in these pages, confirm the current rules with the issuing agency or with a qualified professional who knows your circumstances.

Web addresses are given for the agencies and organizations themselves rather than for individual pages, because individual pages move.

Chapter 5 — The Habits That Build Financial Security

Employer plan matching formulas, vesting schedules, 401(k) and 403(b) contributions, Roth IRA eligibility, and spousal IRAs: Internal Revenue Service, Publication 590-A, Contributions to Individual Retirement Arrangements (IRAs), and the retirement plan pages at irs.gov.

New York 529 plan state income tax deduction, qualified education expenses, and tax-free growth: New York's 529 College Savings Program Direct Plan, and the New York State Department of Taxation and Finance. Deduction limits and rules differ by state.

Chapter 7 — The Power of Consistent Investing

Vanguard Total Stock Market ETF (VTI) and Vanguard Value ETF (VTV): fund objectives and composition drawn from Vanguard prospectuses and fund profiles at vanguard.com. Both funds are named as examples, not as recommendations.

The market decline of 2008 and the recovery that followed: Federal Reserve Board historical data, and the business cycle dates published by the National Bureau of Economic Research.

Chapter 8 — Time, Your Greatest Financial Asset

The comparison between an investor who begins at twenty-five and one who begins at thirty-five is my own calculation. It assumes two hundred dollars contributed from every biweekly paycheck, twenty-six contributions a year, a hypothetical eight percent annual rate compounded biweekly, and all earnings left invested for the full period. It is an illustration of how compounding behaves, not a projection of what any investment will earn.

Chapter 9 — Health Is Part of Wealth

The figure of $185,500: Fidelity Investments, twenty-fifth annual Retiree Health Care Cost Estimate, released July 2026. The estimate applies to a sixty-five-year-old retiring in 2026, assumes enrollment in Original Medicare, Parts A and B, together with Medicare Part D, and excludes long-term care. It represents an increase of 7.5 percent over the prior year's estimate of $172,500.

What Medicare does and does not cover, including its limited coverage of skilled nursing and rehabilitation and its general exclusion of custodial long-term care: Centers for Medicare and Medicaid Services, medicare.gov.

The six-month Medigap open enrollment period, medical underwriting outside that window, and guaranteed issue rights: Centers for Medicare and Medicaid Services, medicare.gov. State protections vary.

Medicaid long-term care eligibility and the five-year lookback period applied to asset transfers: Centers for Medicare and Medicaid Services, medicaid.gov. Eligibility is administered by the states and varies.

Long-term care insurance underwriting, medical qualification, and the effect of purchase age on premiums: National Association of Insurance Commissioners, A Shopper's Guide to Long-Term Care Insurance, naic.org.

Chapter 10 — Building an Emergency Fund

Guidance leaning toward at least six months of living expenses held in a federally insured account: Federal Deposit Insurance Corporation, "Saving for the Unexpected and Your Future," FDIC Consumer Resource Center, fdic.gov.

Deposit insurance coverage limits and account ownership categories: Federal Deposit Insurance Corporation, fdic.gov.

The distinction between a bank money market deposit account, which is federally insured, and a money market mutual fund, which is not: Federal Deposit Insurance Corporation, fdic.gov, and the United States Securities and Exchange Commission, investor.gov.

A lender's ability to reduce or suspend a home equity line of credit: Consumer Financial Protection Bureau, consumerfinance.gov.

Chapter 11 — Insurance, Protecting What You've Built

Replacement cost compared with market value, umbrella liability coverage, uninsured and underinsured motorist coverage, and the policy definitions that govern disability claims: National Association of Insurance Commissioners, naic.org, and the Insurance Information Institute, iii.org.

Chapter 12 — Why Smart People Still Get Money Wrong

The study of more than sixty-six thousand brokerage households: Brad M. Barber and Terrance Odean, "Trading Is Hazardous to Your Wealth: The Common Stock Investment Performance of Individual Investors," Journal of Finance 55, no. 2 (April 2000): 773-806. The study examined

66,465 households holding accounts at a large discount broker between 1991 and 1996, and found that the households trading most actively earned an annual return of 11.4 percent while the market returned 17.9 percent.

Loss aversion: Daniel Kahneman and Amos Tversky, "Prospect Theory: An Analysis of Decision under Risk," Econometrica 47, no. 2 (March 1979): 263-291.

The sunk-cost effect: Hal R. Arkes and Catherine Blumer, "The Psychology of Sunk Cost," Organizational Behavior and Human Decision Processes 35, no. 1 (1985): 124-140.

Confirmation bias: Raymond S. Nickerson, "Confirmation Bias: A Ubiquitous Phenomenon in Many Guises," Review of General Psychology 2, no. 2 (1998): 175-220.

Overconfidence and trading activity: Brad M. Barber and Terrance Odean, "Boys Will Be Boys: Gender, Overconfidence, and Common Stock Investment," Quarterly Journal of Economics 116, no. 1 (February 2001): 261-292.

Chapter 13 – Understanding Social Security Before You Claim

Full retirement age, the permanent reduction for claiming at sixty-two, delayed retirement credits, spousal benefits, survivor benefits and survivor full retirement age, benefits based on a former spouse's record, the annual earnings test, and the adjustment made to withheld benefits once full retirement age is reached: Social Security Administration, including the publication Retirement Benefits and the personalized estimates available through a my Social Security account, ssa.gov.

Deemed filing for individuals born on or after January 2, 1954, and the resulting unavailability of a restricted application for spousal benefits alone: Social Security Administration, ssa.gov.

The limit applied to a survivor benefit when the deceased worker claimed a reduced retirement benefit before full retirement age, generally the greater of 82.5 percent of the worker's primary insurance amount and the amount the worker would have been entitled to receive: Social Security Administration, ssa.gov.

Federal income taxation of up to eighty-five percent of benefits: Internal Revenue Service, Publication 915, Social Security and Equivalent Railroad Retirement Benefits. State treatment of benefits varies.

Chapter 14 — Retirement Is Freedom, Not the End of Purpose

Social connection, mental engagement, physical activity, and a sense of purpose in healthier cognitive aging: National Institute on Aging, nia.nih.gov.

Widowhood as a risk factor for cognitive decline: Timothy Singham, Georgia Bell, Rob Saunders, and Joshua Stott, "Widowhood and Cognitive Decline in Adults Aged 50 and Over: A Systematic Review and Meta-Analysis," Ageing Research Reviews 71 (2021): 101461.

The finding that widowed individuals may maintain the same level of social contact and still report greater loneliness: Rosanne Freak-Poli, Claryn S. J. Kung, Joanne Ryan, and Michael A. Shields, "Social Isolation, Social Support, and Loneliness Profiles Before and After Spousal Death and the Buffering Role of Financial Resources," Journals of Gerontology: Series B 77, no. 5 (May 2022): 956-971.

Chapter 15 — Turning a Lifetime of Savings into a Lifetime of Income

Required minimum distribution ages of seventy-three and seventy-five: the SECURE 2.0 Act of 2022, enacted as Division T of the Consolidated Appropriations Act, 2023, and Internal Revenue Service Publication 590-B.

Roth conversions, the applicable five-year rules, and the absence of lifetime required distributions from a Roth IRA: Internal Revenue Service, Publications 590-A and 590-B.

Annuity contract structures, the dependence of any guarantee on the claims-paying ability of the issuing insurer, and state guaranty association coverage limits: National Association of Insurance Commissioners, naic.org, and the National Organization of Life and Health Insurance Guaranty Associations, nolhga.com.

Sequence-of-returns risk and the durability of withdrawal rates: William P. Bengen, "Determining Withdrawal Rates Using Historical Data," Journal of Financial Planning 7, no. 4 (October 1994): 171-180, together with the substantial body of research that has followed it.

Chapter 16 — Keeping More of What You Earn

The additional ten percent federal tax on early distributions and the exceptions that apply: Internal Revenue Service, Topic No. 557 and Topic No. 558, and Publication 590-B.

The provision commonly called the Rule of 55: Internal Revenue Service, Topic No. 558. It generally applies only to the plan of the employer from which the employee separated from service.

Substantially equal periodic payments under Internal Revenue Code Section 72(t): Internal Revenue Service, Notice 2022-6, and Publication 590-B.

The April 1 deadline for a first required minimum distribution: Internal Revenue Service, Publication 590-B.

The income-related monthly adjustment amount, the two-year lookback on tax return information, and the life-changing event request made on Form SSA-44: Social Security Administration, "Medicare Premiums: Rules for Higher-Income Beneficiaries," ssa.gov, and the Centers for Medicare and Medicaid Services, cms.gov.

Qualified charitable distributions beginning at age seventy and a half, and the annually adjusted limit: Internal Revenue Service, Publication 590-B.

Donating appreciated property, the applicable deduction limits, and substantiation requirements: Internal Revenue Service, Publication 526, Charitable Contributions.

Capital gains and losses, the annual limit on losses deducted against ordinary income, and the wash sale rule: Internal Revenue Service, Topic No. 409, and Publication 550, Investment Income and Expenses.

Withholding, estimated tax payments, and underpayment penalties: Internal Revenue Service, Publication 505, Tax Withholding and Estimated Tax.

Chapter 17 — Teaching the Next Generation About Money

Custodial Roth IRA eligibility, and the rule limiting the contribution to the child's own earned income for the year: Internal Revenue Service, Publication 590-A.

The rollover of unused 529 funds into a Roth IRA, the lifetime limit of thirty-five thousand dollars, the fifteen-year account requirement, and the beneficiary's earned income requirement: the SECURE 2.0 Act of 2022, Section 126.

Housing, higher education, and medical care costs rising faster than overall inflation over long periods: United States Bureau of Labor Statistics, Consumer Price Index detailed expenditure category data, bls.gov.

Chapter 18 — The Legacy You Leave

The requirement that many non-spouse beneficiaries fully distribute an inherited retirement account within ten years, and the exceptions available to eligible designated beneficiaries: the SECURE Act of 2019, and Internal Revenue Service Publication 590-B.

Trusts, durable powers of attorney, healthcare proxies, and the precedence of beneficiary designations over the terms of a will: these are governed by state law and vary considerably. Readers should consult a qualified estate attorney licensed in their own state.

Any error in the description of these sources is mine alone.

About the Author

Jimmy T. Singh, CPA, is a former Corporate Controller, author, independent financial consultant, and private investor with nearly forty years of leadership experience in public accounting, healthcare finance, and executive management. He began his career in public accounting before joining one of the largest not-for-profit home- and community-based health care organizations in the United States, where he advanced from Senior Accountant to Corporate Controller, a role he held for nearly twelve years, later serving as Divisional Controller before leaving corporate life on his own terms.

Since then, he has focused his time on writing, consulting, managing his personal investments, and mentoring young accounting professionals. He is the author of *A Life Well Lived: From a Small Village to a Life of Purpose, Success, and Love* and *The Wealth You Build: A Lifetime of Financial Wisdom*. He also writes *Reflections by Jimmy T. Singh, CPA*, a LinkedIn newsletter on financial wisdom, leadership, and purpose.

He was named a Marquis Who's Who Honored Listee. He holds a BA in Accounting and Finance from Queens College and completed executive studies at Cornell University's ILR School. He lives with his wife on Long Island, New York.

To read more of his writing, visit jimmytsingh.com.

www.ingramcontent.com/pod-product-compliance
Lightning Source LLC
LaVergne TN
LVHW100144061126
851857LV00010B/235